As I See It

Class Warfare: The Only Resort to Right Wing Doom

Egberto Willies is a self-employed software engineer who has always been interested in politics and its ultimate effects on society at large. He is an ardent Liberal that believes tolerance is essential and that political involvement should be a requirement for citizenship. Egberto believes that we must get away from the current policies that reward those who simply move money/capital and produce nothing tangible for our society and that if this is not done, we will become the same as many oligarchic societies where a few are able to accumulate wealth while the rest are left out because it is mathematically impossible to catch up.

Email: egberto@egbertowillies.com
Web: http://egbertowillies.com
Twitter: http://twitter.com/egbertowillies

ISBN-13: 978-1-453-60816-6
ISBN-10: 1-453-60816-8

Contents

Introduction

I am not a Liberal scholar. I am not a Conservative scholar. What I am is a concerned American citizen that while always politically aware, did not become engaged until the troubling times that broke my last straw with our country under the tutelage of a corrupt administration that decided to invade a country that had nothing to do with the vicious attacks we suffered on September 11th, 2001.

While I wanted to speak out forcefully during the build up to the invasion, I felt impotent. These were times when anyone who criticized the administration was subject to repercussions overtly and unfortunately in many instances covertly. I felt that I was back in Panamá during the early years of the government overthrow by Omar Torrijos Herrera[1] when citizens were scared to say anything critical about the government.

Interesting enough the genesis of what I consider the progressive demise of America began with what many taunt as an era of optimism as President Reagan ascended the throne with rhetoric that as incoherent

---

[1] The military dictator that overthrew President Arnulfo Arias of Panamá

as it was appealed to many including myself. I had just arrived in Texas to start my education and loved the semblance of a leader that seemed ready to reward those who wanted to get ahead without government or any other obstacle.

As I see it, we are at a crossroad. We must decide if we are going to continue our ill-fated move whose outcome is evident in every aspect of our life, from an obscenely disproportionate distribution of wealth, to a Free Trade paradigm that will force a lowering of standards for 95% of Americans as our manufacturing and professional service base continue its migration to foreign slave labor markets.

America the Beautiful

I was born in Panamá, Central America. I was always exposed to American history, American government, and American culture as my father and his father worked most of their lives in an area in Panamá called the Canal Zone. This was a strip of land 5 miles wide on either side of the Panamá Canal that was governed by the Americans. An interesting fact is that I was born in the same hospital as Senator John McCain, Coco Solo Hospital[2], of course with much less pampering.

Panamanians working in certain areas for the Americans were either required or had the option to live in the Canal Zone. Given my father's job as a fireman we eventually lived there. As such my first 10 years of schooling was in the Latin American Schools in the Canal Zone where we were educated in both English and Spanish as opposed to the American Schools whose students were taught solely in English, in effect a transposition of America on foreign soil.

---

[2] While Senator John McCain was born on foreign soil while President Barack Obama was born on US Soil proper, is it not ironic that it's the President's citizenship and place of birth being questioned?

While the Latin American schools on the Canal Zone did not have the amenities of the American Schools, we had advantages that did not become evident until the schools were integrated during my last two years of high school. The Latin American schools basic curriculum required Panamanian geography, civics & history, American geography, civics, & history, & world geography and history. Moreover each subject could be taught in either English or Spanish.

I still remember having to remember the nine provinces of Panamá and their capital cities, the 50 states of the United States and their respective capitals, and the capitals of every darn country in the world. Luckily, then we treated the Soviet Union, Yugoslavia, and Czechoslovakia each as one country saving learning 20+ more capitals.

Inasmuch as the standard of living afforded Panamanians living in the Canal Zone was substandard in comparison to that of the Americans, it was higher than most Panamanians. This bought Americans a certain loyalty from Panamanians living in the Canal Zone as well as a loyalty for those who aspired to get a job on the Canal Zone to improve their standard of living.

I remember a particular story my father told me that makes this point. My parents lived in Colón, a city on the Atlantic coast that bordered the Canal Zone. Riots broke out in the city and my father working for the Americans was manning one of the fire trucks to hose down the rioters to prevent them from getting into the Canal Zone. The rioters began threatening the Panamanians working on behalf of the Americans. At that point many Panamanians working for the fire department convinced the Americans to get housing and with that many benefits afforded the Americans in shopping and other services.

From the time I became cognizant of there being an America, I have only known it to be revered not only by me but by most people I knew, Panamanian or foreign. This was not a blind reverence. We were all aware of the evils suffered by the Native Indians, Slaves, Chinese, and others at the hand of America. We however understood that America was atoning and the reality is no country, ethnicity, or race had a monopoly on the mistreatment of others.

America was respected for its power. Moreover there was great admiration of many of its strong leaders like President Abraham Lincoln, President Theodore

Roosevelt[3], President Franklin Roosevelt, President John Kennedy, Reverend Martin Luther King, Malcolm X, George Washington Carver, and a few other true American heroes.

My maternal grandfather immigrated to the United States in the 1950's. He had not returned to Panamá until sometime in the early 1970's when I was really young. To this day I remember picking up his shoes, looking at the soles and telling him, "*Imagine these shoes walked in the United States*". Such were the feelings one had for this land.

In 1976 I wrote a song "America" for the bicentennial celebration of America's independence that was performed by the Dynamites, a band I formed with three of my best friends Roberto Lewis, Alexis Goodridge, and Henry Soley.

---

[3] It must be noted that Theodore Roosevelt's administration instigated the formation of the country of Panamá which was a province of Colombia. When Colombia refused a Canal Treaty he encouraged the new country and immediately signed the Panamá Canal Treaty.

Our high school participated in the celebrations and had many in the Canal Zone government present for the function. The lyrics started with the familiar lyrics of America The Beautiful's chorus and then moved into our celebration of America.

America! America!
God shed his grace on thee
And crown thy good with brotherhood
From sea to shining sea!
...
America. Happy Birthday to you.
We are proud to know, you are 200 years.
We know that you see, You're the land of the free
A land we all love, From sea to shining sea
...Chorus
Oh America, You know we really love America
It is the nation, of the free.

Oh America, Oh America
It's the nation we all love.
...
Your united states. We all contemplate.
A life we all love. A life we dream of.
[chorus]
[JAMMING MUSICAL]

It is important that as Americans we realize that contrary to the narrative we hear mostly on Right Wing radio & television stations, the America most of the world knew in the 20th century post World War II was not an America that foreigners hated "because of their freedom". In fact America was the country most revered. America was the country most wanted to emulate.

America was the country that made things happen. America was skyscrapers, NASA, SkyLab, Grand Canyon, Motown, Michael Jackson, Elvis Presley, a horn of plenty, Hollywood, New York, Ford, Buick, Plymouth. America made things. America innovated. The best from the rest of the world did what it took to get here not to become filthy rich but because America had the resources, the vision, the character that allowed anyone to make it with their work.

America was and is a country in which the sum of its parts unlike any other country in the world is what made it strong. With all of its faults it is that synergy, the composite mental power and diversity from peoples from all over the world that has given it all the resources that made it great. It is the marginalization of the vast majority of these resources that will dictate its demise left to the misguided efforts of the Right Wing.

The Presidents

While our presidents do not have absolute power, they ultimately play a large part in setting the national agenda. Our direction was shaped by the ideology they ultimately brought to the Whitehouse. Inasmuch as Congress plays a major role in legislation, ultimately nothing relatively palatable to the executive branch, the president is generally effected.

The above truth presents a double edge sword in that bad policy can permeate the country for decades. Our current state is proof positive.

Voodoo Economics - Genesis Of Our Demise

Ronald Reagan, the Messiah of the Right Wing was in the right place at the right time. Though a young teenager in 1976, I remember being engaged in the 1976 election. After all, my father, a fanatic of US politics had taped the Congressional hearings on most of my cassette tapes so I was well aware of the corruption that was President Nixon[4]. In my less than schooled mind at that time I saw President Ford as an extension of the Nixon administration and as such I was hoping Jimmy Carter would win[5].

Inasmuch as I believe President Carter was seen worldwide as a positive world over, to many Americans this was not the case. To many Americans President Carter was an ineffective leader because of a gasoline crisis, a stagnant economy, topped off by American hostages being held in Iran. Nothing seemed to go right.

---

[4] As I grew older I actually learned to admire Richard Nixon for many of his policies that today seem so pragmatic, from universal healthcare to talking to our enemies. I am of the firm belief that Nixon got caught for something likely done by many previous and future politicians.

[5] Many people around the world monitor US elections as the outcomes not only affect Americans but foreigners as well.

I came to the United States in 1979 to attend college. I got a music scholarship to play in the Blinn College marching band and jazz band in Brenham, TX[6]. I was new to the country but was well versed in its national politics. Interesting enough, I remember not really understanding the angst of Americans. Things seemed pretty good to me. I got a job in the cafeteria sweeping floors, washing dishes, and doing any odd jobs necessary to make a few bucks.

Then it happened; The Iran Hostage Crisis. Ted Koppell then started counting the days on his new program America Held Hostage later renamed to Nightline. It was that in your face "American held hostage". The writing was on the wall for President Carter even though much was out of his control and he should not have been penalized for it.

Reagan's rhetoric was appealing but made no sense. He promised to reduce government spending but increase military spending, reduce government regulation, reduce income taxes, reduce capital gains

---

[6] The music scholarship was my avenue to the US to get an engineering degree. Opportunity comes in mysterious ways at times.

marginal tax rates, and to balance the budget in three years.

While running against Ronald Reagan in the primaries George Bush Sr. referred to this plan as voodoo economics. George Bush Sr. was right but Ronald Reagan won the primary to become the Republican nominee. George Bush Sr. sold his soul and became Ronald Reagan's Vice-Presidential running mate.

America bought it. Ultimately Reagan won the election and laid the defining map to ensure the ultimate demise of America. I do not believe President Reagan understood the ultimate results of his policies. I do believe the intellectuals in the Right Wing new exactly what the outcome would be, the pilfering of the middle class. The two major tenets of supply side economics practiced by Ronald Reagan, lower taxes that went disproportionately to the rich and Free trade could only lower the standard of living of working Americans as they compete with slave labor and unregulated markets abroad. By definition Free Markets equalizes labor force pricing and the effects are readily visible.

President Reagan like most in the Right Wing believes in supply side economics. The reality is that supply side economics is nothing more than a religion. Unlike most religions it is designed to categorically maximize the wealth of those with capital and the ability to move capital.

The basic tenet of supply side economics is that if you lower taxes on capital gains, other investments, as well as dramatically cut regulation on business that miraculously business will do the right thing to create products and services that people would want. Additionally this philosophy distinctly supports unfettered free markets. In the process somehow tax revenues would increase to cover the loss revenue from the tax cuts.

As an engineer who believes solely in numbers I remain baffled by academic institutions that allow this to be taught. The fallacy that increased taxes necessarily depresses an economy or that lower taxes automatically increase economic activity makes absolutely no sense. What matters in every case is how revenue is spent. Money does not know who spends it, government or Private Corporation or Individuals. If the expenditure is multiplicative increase economic activity occurs, period.

If the government increased taxes to purchase bread from Brazil to feed the poor in America that tax would demonstratively have a negative effect on our economy as all the additional employees hired and supplies purchased for the bread exported to our poor would create economic activity in Brazil while transferring the wealth of Americans overseas.

If the government increased taxes to help feed the poor in America by having more grain purchased from American farmers, more people hired to bake the bread, more ovens, mixers, and equipment purchased from American companies, a self-sustaining multiplicative economic effect occurs.

Government simply lowering taxes does not guarantee that said savings would be reinvested into the economy. As such a marginal increase in economic activity cannot be guaranteed.

When President Reagan came into power, our economy was in shambles. One of the major causes of stagflation, an economic state where we had both high unemployment and high inflation, resulted from the astronomical increases in the price of oil. Stagflation resulted because oil being an indispensible commodity that we could not wean off of rapidly did not lend itself to "market forces" compensating for an alternative in a timely fashion. As such prices went up (inflation) because the underlying indispensible commodity went up and employment went up because of the same underlying mechanism.

After oil price stabilization, what I refer to as effect absorption had occurred, basic Keynesian Economics was responsible for the Reagan Recovery his cohorts cloaked as the success of supply side economics. In effect Keynesian Economics dictates that in times where the private sector is not hiring that the government through deficit spending should be the entity of last resort that employs and purchases to prime economic activity. That is exactly what President Reagan did however in a manner that was less effective than it could have been. President Reagan lowered taxes, increased military spending, and the budget all at the same time. In effect, by lowering taxes and increasing government spending he put money in the hands of people to spend while effecting more spending by the government. The flaw in this method is that had he forgone the tax cuts and invested in infrastructure and education, we would have created wealth for the middle classes as they worked in higher paying jobs, we would have increased our productivity as we built better roads, high speed rails, transmissions & communication systems, and we would have had a more educated populace where the importation of engineers and scientist many corporations claim we need would be home grown.

Of course the wealthy pays the most taxes. However, the marginal propensity to consume of the wealthy is not likely to be excessively dependent on tax rates as it would for those whose disposable income are so much less. It is because of this fact that tax cuts for the upper classes do not return the bang for the buck. Tax cuts for the wealthy in effect becomes the mechanism by which the rich are allowed to accumulate further wealth while the society that collectively provided the cocoon and the ability for their wealth creation is left with meager resources to run said society.

It should be noted that though President Reagan is usually credited with being a great tax cutter, he should better be known as the President that provided obscene tax cuts to the rich (from a marginal tax rate of 70% to 28%). Thereafter he supported the largest tax increase in US history. Taxes now were skewed much less to the wealthy than before. In effect, he increased the tax burden on the middle class while quadrupling the national debt.

Many will view the above statement as a prelude to class warfare. It is far from it. That said class warfare is likely what is needed now to take back our country from the Oligarchs.

There are many groups that have recognized the un-sustainability of our current economic model like United For A Fair Economy[7]. Katrina vanden Heuval, editor of The Nation has a short to the point blog piece[8] that is reflective.

Virtually all policies adopted by President Reagan were a war against the middleclass and working people. Fired air traffic controllers to bust the union and immunize further major labor movements. He changed the tax code to shift more of the tax burden to the middle class. Of course deregulation of the Savings & Loans effected their collapse that was ultimately cleaned up by government, middle class tax dollars.

---

[7] The website for this group can be found at http://blt.ly/bLyu0Y.
[8] Responsible Wealth, Responsible Taxes by Katrina vanden Heuval http://bit.ly/bptvO0

David Stockman, President Reagan's OMB directory and one of the architects of Reagan's economic policy said it best in his article in the New York Times titled Four Deformations Of The Apocalypse.

> *This debt explosion has resulted not from big spending by the Democrats, but instead the Republican Party's embrace, about three decades ago, of the insidious doctrine that deficits don't matter if they result from tax cuts.*

> *In 1981, traditional Republicans supported tax cuts, matched by spending cuts, to offset the way inflation was pushing many taxpayers into higher brackets and to spur investment. The Reagan administration's hastily prepared fiscal blueprint, however, was no match for the primordial forces — the welfare state and the warfare state — that drive the federal spending machine.*

> *Soon, the neocons were pushing the military budget skyward. And the Republicans on Capitol Hill who were supposed to cut spending exempted from the knife most of the domestic budget — entitlements, farm subsidies,*

education, water projects. But in the end it was a new cadre of ideological tax-cutters who killed the Republicans' fiscal religion. (1)

For a President and its Right Wing cohorts that continue to wrap itself in the flag and patriotism, it is ironic that their economic policies have been so disastrous to the country. What is more onerous is their refusal to look at these policies objectively, acknowledge its effects on the middle class and modify policies accordingly. They spend most of their times revising history both literally and through a potent Right Wing echo chamber.

As more challenge the validity of the noise and as the ubiquity of readily available information from reputable sites throughout the Internet is brought to the forefront, the noise machine will go from a potent source of misinformation to a source of political comedy.

President Reagan's policies were ultimately a failure and were the genesis of our current economic demise. To understand the reasons for the demise we must understand that the ideological shift and misrepresentations of the results of Reagan's policies that many Democrats and Republicans latched onto ultimately led us here.

All told if we were to judge President Reagan by his words, any rational person must conclude that he was less than patriotic. After all, his famous quote

> *"Government is not the solution to our problems. Government is the problem."*

is a condemnation of the government being we the people. He disregards the blood that was shed to create our form of representative government that ultimately is controlled by the population. His desire to remove government regulation and reduce government size is in effect a desire for a country that is by the corporation for the corporation. In other words a country controlled by the major corporate shareholders, the wealthy elite.

Voodoo Economics Reversed

I got my American citizenship in 1988. It was the first year that I was going to be able to vote for the President of the United States. I took that responsibility seriously. Governor Dukakis did not impress me with his campaigning. I thought Vice President George Bush was more presidential, more intellectual however aloof. Moreover I expected given his complete understanding of President Reagan's economic policy as Voodoo Economics that irrespective of his pronouncements he would govern fiscally accordingly. I voted for Bush Sr. and he was elected in 1988. Fiscally President Bush Sr. did not disappoint.

Bush Sr. seemed to be always at war with his integrity versus the Right Wing of the party. He was a true patriot. He was a moderate Conservative but a patriot. His rhetoric was Conservative enough to placate enough Republicans while his policies were liberal enough to gain Democratic support. Bush Sr. is the last of the type of Republican our country desperately need.

Bush Sr.'s first nominee to the Supreme Court was David Souter. Bush Sr. had to be cognizant that Souter was a Republican liberal. In fact his opening statement to the Judicial Committee said it all. Souter eloquently displayed the empathy of a liberal in prose.

> When those days on the trial court were over, there were two experiences that I took away with me or two lessons that I had learned, and the lessons remain with me today.

> The first lesson, simple as it is, is that whatever court we are in, whatever we are doing, whether we are on a trial court or an appellate court, at the end of our task some human being is going to be affected. Some human life is going to be changed in some way by what we do, whether we do it as trial judges or whether we do it as appellate judges, as far removed from the trial arena as it is possible to be.

> The second lesson that I learned in that time is that if, indeed, we are going to be trial judges, whose rulings will affect the lives of other people and who are going to change their lives by what we do, we had better use every power

of our minds and our hearts and our beings to get those rulings right.[9]

It was evident that in replacing Justice William J Brennan, a staunch liberal, President Bush Sr. had no intention in shifting the balance of the Supreme Court.

I can only imagine the internal disgust Bush Sr. felt with the performance of Clarence Thomas, his second appointment to the Supreme Court to replace Justice Thurgood Marshall. I can only surmise that given that Clarence Thomas was the Chairman of the Equal Employment Opportunity Commission Bush Sr. may have thought he would display Souter's pragmatism and not a fanatical Right Wing ideology once elevated to a position of such responsibility.

President Bush Sr.'s pragmatism led him to break his promise of "no new taxes". He was never forgiven by the Right Wing for this. I find it ironic since President Reagan signed many tax increases and paid no real political price for it.

President Bush Sr.'s broken promise was the beginning of our path to America's balance budget.

---

[9] David Souter Opening Statement to Judiciary Committee
http://bit.ly/dnkhMo

Though I consider President Bush Sr. one of our better presidents he did err in invading the country of my birth, Panamá. The Right Wing has always been opposed to the Panamá Canal Treaty signed between President Jimmy Carter and General Omar Torrijos Herrera, the then leader of the Panamanian government.

After the death of Torrijos (many believe at the hand of the CIA with the assistance of Noriega), Manuel Antonio Noriega became the leader of Panamá. Noriega was on the CIA payroll for many years. In fact there was a quid pro quo that allowed Noriega to run his drug trafficking and laundering shenanigans in exchange for intelligence both on the Sandinistas in Nicaragua and other Latin American issues. As the United States' drug use problem increased the War on Drugs made continued support for Noriega untenable.

President Reagan in his desire to oust Noriega froze Panamanian accounts in US banks and prohibited US companies from doing business in Panama. Because the US dollar is the common currency in Panamá it crippled the economy and the population suffered without any effect on Noriega's ability to survive.

After several failed US instigated coups, President Bush Sr. finally invaded Panamá to capture Noriega. He simultaneously attacked the three largest cities, Panamá City, Colón, and David. I can still remember the fear in my father's voice when we were able to make contact. He spoke of helicopters flying overhead and missiles indiscriminately being fired not only on military targets but several high rise government housing buildings. He lived next to Colón. Many were sure that the stealth fighter was tested in combat there. Of course Panamá had no real Air Force so one must wonder.

Most devastating was the attack at Noriega's headquarters in Chorrillo, an area in Panamá City which was surrounded by many apartments, home to thousands. This whole area was bombed and burned to the ground. The US military reported civilian deaths on the order of 1000. Attorney General Ramsey Clark claimed more than 4,000. The likely number is greater than 10,000 given the population density in the areas attacked throughout the country. Moreover after the initial invasion many more Panamanians attempting to pass several blockades were killed because of language barriers and trigger happy soldiers.

I specifically address this invasion as a low point for President Bush Sr. for one reason. Right Wing thinking leads to poor analysis of problems. It always seek short term brute force solutions that ultimate create many more problems than they solve.

President Bush Sr. ultimately got his man Noriega but at what cost. How would you feel if many of the dead were relatives; a mother, a father, a brother, a son, a daughter, a friend, a niece, a nephew? The invasion created bad precedence.

1. Just as flawed as is supply side economics, trying to stop US drug usage by attacking its supply has never worked. The drug problem is an American problem that the rest of the world is willing to supply. It follows the American tenet of supply and demand. We must solve the drug problem at home by legalizing drugs, regulating, and taxing it thus removing the incentive for distribution criminality.
2. No country has the right to arrest the leader of another country. What would our reaction be if some other country attempted to arrest President Bush Sr. for having effected the

innocent deaths of the thousands of Panamanians that perished.

3. America lost the moral authority to stop any other invader country from invading another when said country is perceived to be influencing the behavior of citizens of the invader country even if said citizens are acting on their own volition.

The optics is horrible and it deteriorated people's impressions of the United States' government for a while. It must be stated that most people in the world make the distinction between the average American and the government in effect as they know it is temporary. They know that America is a strong Democracy in which governments will change and ultimately policies will change. This is one of the reasons President Obama's candidacy and presidency was yearned for around the world. It was a perceived real change in US policy.

The debt we owe President Bush Sr. is returning to reality. Reagan's perceived success was built on the smoke and mirrors of policies that were mathematically mutually exclusive.

The Return Of Fiscal Responsibility

While I voted for President Bush Sr. in 1988, I could not support him given that the GOP was on a steady move to the Right. Moreover, his proven will to invade an independent country gave me pause. I voted for President Bill Clinton in the 1992 elections. President Clinton humble upbringing was a good indication that he would be an empathetic president. He understood all Americans because he lived among them all. Being extremely intelligent with the ability to communicate was exactly the president we needed.

President Clinton knew that the budget deficit was going to be a large drag on our economy. His singular most important accomplishment was signing the Omnibus Budget Reconciliation Bill of 1993[10]. This bill was passed without a single Republican vote in Congress[11]. Republicans as usual stated that the bill would destroy our economy. The bill raised taxes on the wealthiest 1.2% of taxpayers, cut taxes for 15 million low income families, and cut taxes on up to 90% of small businesses. It also created a 35% income

---

[10] Omnibus Budget Reconciliation Bill of 1993:
http://bit.ly/cUV8PR
[11] House Vote: http://bit.ly/9uTHY9 Senate Vote:
http://bit.ly/bAM3CF

tax rate for corporations. It is this bill that laid the foundation for America to get its house back in fiscal order. It got the budget ultimately balanced.

Rather than causing an economic collapse, his administration was marked by a historic economic growth[12]. Average growth under President Reagan was 2.8% while it was 4.0% under President Clinton. 20.7 million Jobs, the most under any administration were created. Unemployment hit the lowest rate in 30 years. Inflation was the lowest since the 1960's averaging 2.5%.

President Clinton also got the Family and Medical Leave Act of 1993 passed and the Children's Health Insurance Program (CHIP). What the Clinton administration proved is that it is possible to be socially conscious, develop policies that assist the middleclass, and by taxing wealth and income in a balanced fashion we can have a robust economy that every living American can actually be a part of.

Inasmuch as President Clinton's Administration was instrumental in creating a robust economy, its support for Free Trade and the passage of the Financial

---

[12] Clinton's Historic Economic Growth: http://bit.ly/a1urLP

Services Modernization Act of 1999 added fertilizer for our current economic failures. It was as if late in his administration he channeled President Reagan's deregulation vision.

Free Trade is nothing but a license to commoditize labor which is exactly what has occurred. It made labor just a line on a ledger without taking the human condition into consideration.

Countries like the United States attempt to be environmentally responsible and provide good working conditions for its workers. Unless all countries participating in a Free Trade market have comparable labor laws & environmental laws, the American worker would always be at a disadvantage and unable to compete. Moreover, it is impossible to compete effectively with countries whose standards of living are orders of magnitude lower than ours. Mathematically the country with the higher standard of living must fall or the standard of living of the foreign country must grow or a combination of both. It is evident that with the loss of much of our manufacturing base where a living wage was generally paid relative to foreign countries we are in the process of reaching this sad equilibrium.

President Clinton's signing of the Gramm-Leach-Bliley Act, better known as the Financial Modernization Act[13] which allowed insurance companies, commercial banks, investment banks, and securities firms to coexist as one entity was an arrangement that opened the door to fraud and market manipulation. In effect this law removed the protections instituted by the Glass-Steagall Act of 1933 specifically designed to prevent the shenanigans that the effective repeal of this act caused. The signature of this Right Wing developed bill, the Free Trade bill, and the disastrous economic policy of the president that followed President Clinton must be considered the biggest financial blunder of our country and left unchecked will be the demise of our country.

President Clinton's second term was marred by the Monica Lewinsky sex scandal. While the Right Wing gloated in its ability to impeach the President for his less than truthful assertions of his relationship with Lewinsky, it was the country that was hurt by the lack of progress on many fronts while the media and lawmakers were enthralled in the story as oppose to concern of laws to improve middleclass American's

---

[13] Financial Modernization Act: http://bit.ly/9t7vJh

lives. In the process ironically the moral depravity of mostly those on the Right Wing came to the forefront and many of their careers were irreparably damaged unlike that of President Clinton whose ongoing humanitarian deeds atoned for any perceived negative.

Absent this scandal it is doubtful that President Clinton would have acquiesced to the type of policies in his second term that effectively codified legalized gambling with investor dollars culminating with the 2008 financial collapse.

Fiscal Insanity Revisited And Expanded

The 2000 election was pivotal. It was a fork in the road and while Americans by a majority chose Al Gore to be the President we had an obscene corruption of democracy to install President George Bush Jr. as president. An advance country like the United States by now should have abolished the Electoral College. In effect the Electoral College is there to decide if the President elected by Americans will actually be the president that serves.

I personally believe there was more to the 2000 election than reported. From the butterfly ballot in West Palm Beach that confused the elderly Democrats and cost Al Gore a loss of over 6000 votes, to the outright unprecedented order by the supreme court to stop counting, and to Gore almost meek like acceptance of a bullied defeat.

President Bush Jr. was a likeable person. Unfortunately he neither had the intellect, curiosity, or temperament to be president of the world's most powerful country. As such it is evident he was in control of neither his domestic nor especially his foreign policy and for most of his presidency was nothing but a figure head with a cowboy disposition. He served as a conduit to implement Right Wing Think Tank policy papers.

9/11 presented a blank canvas for the "president" to shape an alternate reality and put unabated Right Wing policies into effect. In the process we loss support of most of the world and it drew us into an unprecedented financial crisis second only to the Great Depression.

President Bush Jr.'s reign can only be categorized as an abject failure.

- His initial response to the 9/11 terrorist attack was that of a scared president as he spoke to an elementary school class. Thereafter his handlers were able to convert this attack into an excuse to invoke laws (The Patriot Act[14]) more in line with communist China than that of the US. Anyone speaking up against the administration corrupt policy was silenced or damaged. Phones could be tapped indiscriminately with little checks and balances. Anyone could be arrested and denied access to legal representation. During these years I was

---

[14] Final text of Patriot Act: http://bit.ly/comZMo

legitimately scared to express opinions and facts that were contrary to the administration. I had many websites under proxies in an attempt to add a level of obscurity to my blogging. It was like living in one of the dictatorships in Latin America.

- The President lost the opportunity to lead in reducing greenhouse gas emissions by opposing the Kyoto Protocol.
- He attempted to amend the Clean Air Act with the environmental sounding name Clear Skies Act of 2003 which actually would have increased pollutants.
- He opposed real stem cell research.
- His response to Hurricane Katrina showed ineptitude rarely evident from a US president. While the media showed the vast suffering across the Gulf Coast he seemed oblivious to the colossal devastation.
- He effected the largest tax cut, 1.35 trillion dollars, in US history while increasing spending dramatically. When Treasury Secretary Paul O'Ncill opposed the policy on the grounds it would undermine social security and

dramatically increase the budget deficit he was eventually summarily dismissed.

- Inflation adjusted median income between 2000 and 2007 dropped by $1,175, a direct result of the transfer of wealth from the middle class to the wealthy via tax cuts that benefited mostly the rich.
- Poverty increased substantially.
- Bush Jr. entered office with the Dow Jones average at 10,587. It zoomed to 14,000 on the bubble created by bad fiscal and monetary policies. By the time he left the Dow Jones was at 7949.
- He instituted No Child Left Behind that while in theory should close the education gap between the rich and poor students has resulted in teachers teaching to a test as opposed to having students engaged in real learning.
- President Bush Jr. had the least number of jobs created under his administration than any other President since the Great Depression.

President	Jobs created
George W. Bush Sr.	3.0 million
Bill Clinton	23.1 million
George H.W. Bush Jr.	2.5 million
Ronald Reagan	16.0 million
Jimmy Carter	10.5 million
Gerald Ford	1.8 million
Richard Nixon	9.4 million
Lyndon Johnson	11.9 million
John F. Kennedy	3.6 million
Dwight Eisenhower	3.5 million
Harry Truman	8.4 million

The chart above seems to corroborate that when Keynesian economic principles are in effect relative to our current economic implementation more jobs are created. In fact even while Reagan claimed to be a small government conservative, Keynesian principles governed his economic activity. Tax cuts without reciprocal budgetary cuts is no different that out right deficit spending to prime an economy. The only difference is that it rewards the wealthy In a progressive tax system.

By the 2004 campaign I thought that America would have seen the fraud that the current administration was. Just before the election I wrote a blog entry at one of my then proxy sites (http://politicaltruths.info) that I thought most Americans were feeling.

> **President Bush** Jr.**'s policies are immoral.**
>
> *Morality is a touchy subject. After all, who defines it? Many reporters as well as Republicans are saying that this election was the moral values election. Does that imply that Bush Jr. is moral and Kerry immoral or less than moral? The fact is that they are both wrong. Ironically during the Republican convention Bush Jr. showcased the "immoral" ones (Rudolph Giuliani & Arnold Schwarzenegger).*
>
> *Morality is a very dangerous issue. One should never assume their morals to be superior to another less they set themselves up for the boomerang's return.* **Bush Jr. however has opened the door for one to judge his policies' "morality" on relative terms.** *Many Americans believed that in Bush Jr. they would be getting a more "moral" president. Ironically when looking at Bush Jr.'s issues through clear lens as*

opposed to the fog of his political machine, we see not only a president with "immoral" issues but a president that will cause physical and financial harm to those that are least able to defend themselves.

- *It is immoral to send our soldiers to die on false pretenses.*
- *It is immoral that the richest country on the earth does not provide health care for all of it's citizens.*
- *It is immoral to pass unabated wealth from generation to generation by eliminating the inheritance tax (death tax)*
- *It is immoral to privatize social security a program that should not be dependent on the whims of the stock market.*
- *Is it moral that a family that works everyday will pay more taxes on income made from working than a person who played golf all day but made that same amount of income from dividends?*
- *Is it moral that drug companies are allowed to make large profits on*

medicine while a large percentage of our tax dollars pay for research?

- *It is immoral to run ever growing budget deficits while cutting taxes for those who have prospered the most.*
- *It is immoral to disparage one that has spilled blood for their country while having evaded required service himself.*
- *It is immoral that one cannot practice religion or the absence thereof without government interference.*
- *It is immoral that new laws are allowing more pollution to the environment.*
- *It is immoral to put a woman's body under government control irrespective of her health.*
- *It is immoral to disallow any loving pair from forming a loving relationship.*

Little did I know that fear was much more powerful that morality. The Bush Jr. Administration new exactly how to scare Americans into believing that it was there policies keeping us safe and should not take a chance on electing John Kerry, a decorated Vietnam veteran.

After the Bush Jr. victory I was flabbergasted. My first thought was the country could not survive his unsound economic policy and his destructive foreign policy. The day after the election I wrote the following on my blog.

Give President George Bush Jr. Everything He Wants

Many progressive liberals are very upset with George Bush Jr.'s legitimate victory for President of the United States. They cannot believe that with one of the poorest domestic and foreign records of accomplishment that he could possibly be reelected. Bush Jr.'s political machine was exceptional in translating all of their opponent's strengths to weaknesses. As mentioned in a previous blog it is amazing that Bush Jr. who did not serve could classify Kerry as the weak one. How can Bush Jr., a President with the largest budget deficit seriously classify any opponent as too liberal.

This election is over and progressives must decide how to work under an increasingly right wing administration and a congress that is leaning more to the right. It must first be acknowledged that the country is really moderate but was coerced into the politicians it elected. Smoke and mirrors can be very convincing by a generally trusting population. This will be expanded further in a future blog entry.

Progressives have two choices. They can fight on principle as Bush brings his agenda to congress and stall the process. This approach is completely flawed and will likely effect a further loss of progressives in both the House and the Senate as the right wing will use the same tactics used in this election to lay blame on the country's failure on those in the opposition.

The other alternative is to let Bush Jr. have everything that he wants. The Bush Jr.'s agenda will be a great success for a small percent of the population but will be a dismal failure for the masses. It will make the oligarchic system now prevalent in Russia seem innocuous. At that point Americans will decide if they are willing to accept that massive transfer of wealth and freedom or elect progressives that will set things right.

The country will be set back for several years while digging out of the financial and social mess. This however should lead to several decades of governance by progressives as Bush Jr.'s disaster will form an integral part of the consciousness of millions for decades to come. The motto will be "Do you want to return to the Bush Jr. years?"

My prediction was more accurate for the 2008 election than I could have ever dreamed of. Unfortunately Americans gullibility index is arguably still above average.

The Return Of Sanity

During the 2008 primary elections I was an original supporter of Hillary Clinton. My major issue was competence and Healthcare Reform. I knew that First Lady Hillary Clinton new all the ins and outs of the issue and my initial thought was that she knew the pitfalls and would probably be able to avoid them. As I read her posted Healthcare Proposal next to Barack Obama's proposal it was clear that while hers was more comprehensive because it included mandates from the beginning, it was unlikely to even get a hearing. I believe that mandating that all have insurance is a must lest the system would be abused by those who would only secure insurance when they knew they would need it; however we needed to let Congress see the light as they drafted the legislation and computed it as opposed to it being articulated upfront.

Reading New York Times Op-Ed Columnist/Economist Paul Krugman really was instrumental in me warming to President Obama's plan.

> *"But while it's easy to see how the Clinton plan could end up being eviscerated, it's hard to see how the hole in the Obama plan can be*

repaired. Why? Because Mr. Obama's campaigning on the health care issue has sabotaged his own prospects."[15]

While many would view those words as a negative I viewed them as the very reason Obama's plan stood a chance. In political parlance, he could point to a plan somewhat left of his which could have insulated him from some criticisms on the margin. It was not difficult then to live with his Healthcare Reform plan as ultimately it would be modified going forward and there may have been a left buttress as a starting point.

I was already a bit perturbed with some of the overtones from former President Clinton's dismissal of Obama's primary victory in South Carolina by equating it to then Jesse Jackson's victory a few years back. Clinton is a very intelligent man and I am sure even though I believe he does not have a prejudice bone in his body, he was willing to use subliminal racial inflections to taint Obama's victory. Though I supported Mrs. Clinton, no one could equate Obama's politics with Jackson's. There were many more relevant comparisons.

---

[15] Paul Krugman Op-Ed in NY Times Published Feb 4th, 2008 Titled: Clinton, Obama, Insurance

I made my break from Hillary in February though I was still not sure if Obama could break the "racial barrier" and win. Ironically, I was not sure Obama was going to win until I heard a report of one of Obama's canvassers going to the home of a white blue collar guy and the wife called out asking the husband who they were voting for. The man said "I am voting for the nigger". It was evident the guy was likely racist. However things were so bad, he had heard the same things from guys that looked the same, why not try something else. Why not vote a guy promising a change from how things were for so long. Struggles have a way of bringing on a certain maturity. At that point he realized he did not have to like the person for whatever reason, he just needed someone whose policies was in his interest this time.

In 2008 many blue collar workers were already suffering in silence for years. While the stock markets and the real estate markets were booming, these guys' were methodicly watching their jobs being exported with no end in sight. Ultimately it is this sentiment that provided President Obama's part of his winning margin. The stars aligned for him.

When one dissects President Obama's major platform points, it was a winning message not only in rhetoric but if implemented would lay the ground work for revitalizing America.

The platform though not specifically articulated as stated below was evident from many of his stumps.

- Provide substantial assistance to educate Americans both for professional jobs as well as trade jobs.
- Enact Universal Healthcare to ensure that everyone has a stake and pays into healthcare of the country in order to sure up Medicare & Medicaid which would substantially reduce the structural budget deficit caused by these programs.
- Return to a more progressive tax code that rewards work and not manipulation of capital and thus mitigating the massive wealth theft of the middleclass into the hands of the wealthy.
- Invest and assist in expanding the renewable energy industry to reduce our dependence on foreign oil which assist in improving our environment, slow down climate change, reduce our imbalance of trade, and create millions of jobs.
- Reform Wall Street to protect the consumer from the daily thievery that occurs with the

creation of "legally fraudulent" instruments and from price manipulation.

The implementation of that platform brings equity to America not by redistribution but by fairness and by wealth acquisition based on deeds and not false attributes, luck, and ill-structured defined government policy.

If the ground work of these policies is laid America has hope. If the Right Wing is allowed to derail the direction the voters have set forth with their well-oiled strategic misinforming echo chamber, there will be no one to blame but the voter's gullibility index.

Let's Talk Economy

When I came to America in 1979 to attend college I had very little knowledge of economics. At 18 I knew nothing about the stock market, taxes, supply, demand, money, or the interactions thereof. As an engineering student economics was not a part of the curriculum either. As an avid news geek, I remember hearing terms like inflation, stagflation, Dow Jones Average, and all these other economic terms. I wanted to learn.

I decided to take an Economics 101 class. The class was an eye opener. It is there that I learned about supply and demand. I remember one of the first questions the professor asked was what would happen to the price of a product if there was a lot of demand for some particular product. In my naivety I said the price of the product would fall since the person or company selling the product would have made enough money to cover expenses and could then afford to lower the price. I just could not help but feel that increasing the price for something that was selling well was ethical. Well I learned fast that the free enterprise system as designed operated differently and that pricing was actually how we maintained a somewhat balance on supply and demand.

If Company "A" has a product, they can increase the price of that product just to the point where its price times its volume less expenses to make the product causes a drop in overall profits for that particular product. A product price that generates a profit will ultimately cause a Company "B", Company "C", and so on to start making a similar product and likely price their product lower than Company "A" in order to appeal to some of Company "A"'s customers. Company "A" will be forced to lower their prices to prevent the other companies from taking all their customers for that product.

The above scenario is known as competition and in a free enterprise system free of corruption it is self-balancing, self-regulating, and efficient. In a free enterprise system you have the freedom to create virtually any product or service that you believe a demand would exist for. Demand for what you, an entrepreneur has to offer will determine if your product or service would be profitable and profitability of that product or service will likely determine if others are likely to offer similar product and services to compete with you. This is good for our society all around because competition will keep prices of any product or service more affordable while preventing the concentration of accumulated wealth (excessive profits) in the hands of a few. It is a system that when implemented fairly works for all those who want to produce, create, or be entrepreneurial.

Capitalism Just Not Working For Most

Unfortunately our free enterprise system is not working as it should for many reasons, all bad for the average American entrepreneur. Many equate free enterprise with capitalism. It is my contention that our brand of capitalism will cause the demise of free enterprise and left to its own devices will eventually make every American a unit of labor competing with every unit of labor overseas. We are in the process of becoming indentured servants to the corporation, a working commodity.

Those afforded the ability to gain the most from American innovativeness are no longer the innovators; they are no longer the entrepreneurs. We have become a society that rewards those who move capital and have the ability to cater laws to their benefit. We reward a class of people that provide no real tangible service or product of value proportional to their earnings or wealth.

The wealth and income disparity in the country is not an accident. There are many systemic reasons why this disparity will continue. As long as we have a Right Wing misinformation engine that remains effective in indoctrinating a large percentage of the population to vote policy makers into office that ultimately pass laws that is against their own financial interest, the trend will continue. The following chart shows the progressive decline in wealth of the bottom 80% of the US population.

Total Net Worth[16]

	Top 1 percent	Next 19 percent	Bottom 80 percent
1983	33.80%	47.50%	18.70%
1989	37.40%	46.20%	16.50%
1992	37.20%	46.60%	16.20%
1995	38.50%	45.40%	16.10%
1998	38.10%	45.30%	16.60%
2001	33.40%	51.00%	15.60%
2004	34.30%	50.30%	15.30%
2007	34.60%	50.50%	15.00%

The data illustrates clearly that the vast majority of Americans are not only treading water but falling behind. It is not difficult to empirically figure out the reasons based on the experiences of working people one encounters daily. While worker productivity

---

[16] Reprinted with permission from UCSC Prof. G. William Domhoff (http://bit.ly/9id1wi)

increases, said increase is not reflected in their increase in wages. Instead increased productivity serves as a feather in the cap of the CEOs who reap the benefit with ever increasing salaries. The chart below shows that CEOs salaries over the last several decades have not only increased faster than corporate profits, but more than the S&P index as well as the average worker by several orders of magnitude. Sadly, the minimum wage fared even worst.

Relative Rate of Increase of Salaries[17]

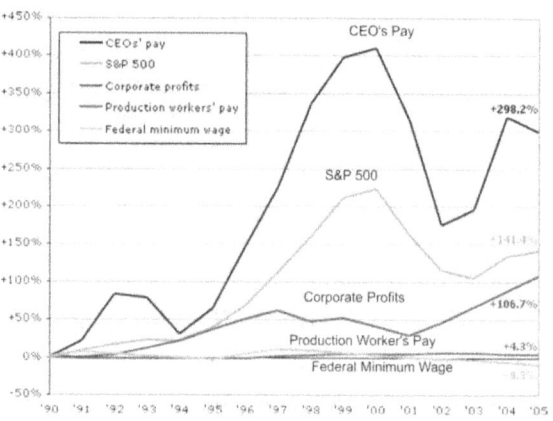

A Capitalist system that allows the inequities in wealth and income as illustrated is unsustainable. If a system

[17] Reprinted with permission from UCSC Prof. G. William Domhoff (http://bit.ly/9id1wi)

is such that it produces these results then it is a failed system. The inequity growth rate is codified in our system specifically because of the laws our duly elected politicians have passed at our behest based on completely false propaganda promoted by the Right and condoned by both Democrats and Republican.

What Is Wrong With Our Brand Of Capitalism?

I am using the term Capitalism to describe our free market economic system in its totality. None of these parts can be disassociated; Financial System, Taxation, Patent Law, Military Spending, Free Trade, and Government Social Services.

Note that while Military Spending and Government Social Services fall under the taxation portion of our system their proportions of the national budget have their own gravity. They are better commented on separately as all other spending pales in comparison. This is our market.

Financial System

The American Financial System is an unnecessarily complex system. This complexity provides for the employment of a group of highly paid individuals who provide no important service or value to society. Their income is simply derived from the manipulation of capital, the manipulation of money. The leaders of this industry create a myriad of financial instruments that they claim make capital available for the growth of business.

The reality is that the financial system does not need to be complex at all. In very simplified terms the basic financial services needed by a company are:

- Investment Capital
- Loans
- Insurance

The basic financial procedure for creating a sandwich shop should be no different than creating an oil company. Assuming you are not independently wealthy, opening a sandwich shop may require a loan from a bank to purchase your freezers, cookers, steam table, etc. A prudent bank will review your business plan and based on your perceived ability to pay back the loan will charge you an interest rate consummate with your risk. The bank likely got the money to lend you from investors in the bank as well as other businesses with deposits in the bank[18]. The bank should ideally make its profits from its fees and interest you pay on your loan.

Alternatively you could just as well get investors that provide you the capital to start your shop. You would provide your investors with stocks in your company. The investors provide you money. You pay the investors some agreed upon quarterly dividend.

You would likely purchase property insurance, personal liability insurance, health insurance, etc. from an insurance company. Insurance companies' get their capital from risk based premiums and investors who make a bet that total insurance payouts to businesses will be less than all premiums taken in.

---

[18] I will not get into the complex role the Federal Reserve plays in the banking game as it is beyond the scope of this book's intent. Suffice it to say that our system would be better served by a nationalized banking system where tax payer dollar is never transferred to private banking and the Federal Reserve becomes a "real" central bank.

Establishing a large oil company should follow the same procedure however on a larger scale. There is no magic. While the above is an overly simplistic overview of establishing a company, the point I want to illustrate is the simplicity that should be the business/financial sector interface.

The titans of our financial systems created a system known as the stock market that buys and sells the stocks investors purchased in companies. In other words the stock the sandwich shop sold to investor "A" for let's say $100,000 could be sold on the stock market to investor "B" for $120,000 or $90,000 or $50,000 or whatever he/she is willing to pay for it. The stock broker who is facilitating the sale between investor "A" and investor "B" makes a commission every time that stock is traded/sold/purchased. This process is a good thing in that it gives an investor the ability to turn their stock into money/cash if they need it for whatever reason. The stock broker is providing a service in finding a buyer for the stock somebody wants to sell.

The corruption of this elegant system comes about with the creation of financial instruments by those in the investment banking industries that have nothing to do with creating companies or jobs. These instruments in effect turn the stock market into nothing more than a slot machine. It is tantamount to legalize gambling. As stated by economist Ph.D. Simon Johnson:

> ... The boom began with the Reagan years, and it only gained strength with the deregulatory policies of the Clinton and George W. Bush Jr. administrations. Several other factors helped fuel the financial industry's ascent. Paul Volcker's monetary policy in the 1980s, and the increased volatility in interest rates that accompanied it, made bond trading much more lucrative. The invention of securitization, interest-rate swaps, and credit-default swaps greatly increased the volume of transactions that bankers could make money on. And an aging and increasingly wealthy population invested more and more money in securities, helped by the invention of the IRA and the 401(k) plan. Together, these developments vastly increased the profit opportunities in financial services.

> ... From 1973 to 1985, the financial sector never earned more than 16 percent of domestic

corporate profits. In 1986, that figure reached 19 percent. In the 1990s, it oscillated between 21 percent and 30 percent, higher than it had ever been in the postwar period. This decade, it reached 41 percent. Pay rose just as dramatically. From 1948 to 1982, average compensation in the financial sector ranged between 99 percent and 108 percent of the average for all domestic private industries. From 1983, it shot upward, reaching 181 percent in 2007.

The great wealth that the financial sector created and concentrated gave bankers enormous political weight—a weight not seen in the U.S. since the era of J.P. Morgan (the man). In that period, the banking panic of 1907 could be stopped only by coordination among private-sector bankers: no government entity was able to offer an effective response. But that first age of banking oligarchs came to an end with the passage of significant banking regulation in response to the Great Depression; the reemergence of an American financial oligarchy is quite recent. (2)

Most of these instruments are created solely to make money off of money, providing absolutely no value to production in our society. Case in point is a credit derivative known as the Credit Default Swap (CDS). This instrument was instrumental in the collapse of 2008 that brought us to the brink of a Depression.

High risk investors bought high risks investments like mortgages or any other type of financial investment. They then purchased Credit Default Swaps on these. In the event these investments failed, the Credit Default Swap would make them whole. In effect the Credit Default Swap is an insurance policy on an investment that will pay the face value of the investment if the underlying investment fails. The problem is that Credit Default Swaps are unregulated unlike insurance companies. As such investment banks had no real rules to abide by on these. For all practical purposes the premiums they collected for the Credit Default Swaps were just considered profits as they acted like the investments would never fail. When investments began failing the cascading effect was equivalent to the tumbling of a house of cards.

Many attempt to indoctrinate Americans to the ideology that the private sector knows best, must be left with as little regulation as possible, and must be taxed minimally. As stated by Nobel Prize Economist Paul Krugman:

> *... America emerged from the Great Depression with a tightly regulated banking system, which made finance a staid, even boring business. Banks attracted depositors by providing convenient branch locations and maybe a free toaster or two; they used the money thus attracted to make loans, and that was that.*

> *... Even during the "go-go years," the bull market of the 1960s, finance and insurance together accounted for less than 4 percent of G.D.P. The relative unimportance of finance was reflected in the list of stocks making up the Dow Jones Industrial Average, which until 1982 contained not a single financial company.*

> *It all sounds primitive by today's standards. Yet that boring, primitive financial system serviced an economy that doubled living standards over the course of a generation.*

After 1980, of course, a very different financial system emerged. In the deregulation-minded Reagan era, old-fashioned banking was increasingly replaced by wheeling and dealing on a grand scale. The new system was much bigger than the old regime: On the eve of the current crisis, finance and insurance accounted for 8 percent of G.D.P., more than twice their share in the 1960s. By early last year, the Dow contained five financial companies — giants like A.I.G., Citigroup and Bank of America. (2)

The titans of finance attempt to make one believe that they know what is best for the economy. The reality is every time these titans of finance have failed, they have been bailed out in some form by the American tax payer. Moreover, the disastrous effects always cause a significant segment of the American population financial stress while those who created the failure are left mostly whole.

Middleclass Americans were told that a large part of the demise of the real estate market was caused by their irresponsibility. They were told that they purchased more house than they could afford. Interesting enough, these are the same titans of finance that created the No Doc or Low Doc loans. There is only one reason to create loans of this type. The intent was to ensure the loan would be made irrespective of the borrower being able to pay it back. This was done because the banks knew they would only hold those loans for a short period of time. These loans were turned into instruments I refer to as quasi fraudulent securities. They were packetized and sold on the market as investment grade bonds. Rating agencies became a part of the fraud.

Worst was that these investment products were then "insured" via the other instrument created by the titans of finance namely the credit default swap. When people stopped paying on their loans, and for many, when they never paid on their loans, the bonds lost their value. At that point the credit default swap should have made investors of those bonds whole. But these unregulated default swaps for all practical purposes had no real reserves behind them so there was no money in escrow or reserve to pay the defaulting bonds.

The scenario is worse than gambling. Gambling is at least honest in that every bet is based on some spread and paid out on said spreads. The money is there to pay. What the titans of finance did was plain and simply legal robbery. After all, the government had no real regulation to prohibit what they were doing.

When it was time to start covering all the failing bonds, given that there was no capital to pay for these, the government had to step in to prevent a cascading worldwide collapse as the trillions of bonds and securities that would eventually become worthless would have been cataclysmic.

It is ironic that these titans of finance, who generally despise government involvement, would need or come to the government for a bailout. These guys are simply not as smart as they would have many believe.

The narrative of the irresponsible middle class American defaulting on his mortgage was embedded in the psyche of America. In fact many middle class Americans are resentful as they themselves struggle with mortgages that are under water. Turns out that as reported by the New York Times:

> *The housing bust that began among the working class in remote subdivisions and quickly progressed to the suburban middle class is striking the upper class in*

privileged enclaves like this one in Silicon Valley.

Whether it is their residence, a second home or a house bought as an investment, the rich have stopped paying the mortgage at a rate that greatly exceeds the rest of the population.

More than one in seven homeowners with loans in excess of a million dollars are seriously delinquent, according to data compiled for The New York Times by the real estate analytics firm CoreLogic.

By contrast, homeowners with less lavish housing are much more likely to keep writing checks to their lender. About one in 12 mortgages below the million-dollar mark is delinquent.

Though it is hard to prove, the CoreLogic data suggest that many of the well-to-do are purposely dumping their financially

> *draining properties, just as they would any*
> *sour investment.* (4)

The rich defaulting on a mortgage is tantamount to a responsible investment decision but for a middle class American family it is a display of irresponsibility.

Taxation

On April 7th, 2010 , a week before Tax Day, an Associated Press writer released an incendiary article titled *"Nearly Half of US Households Escape Fed Income Tax"* . This was fodder for the Right Wing who blasted links to the articles in emails across America. Every conservative friend emailed me the article with the intent of showing that half of Americans were simply free loaders that the rest of us took care of. It never occurred to most that firstly, these people pay many other taxes including sales taxes, property taxes, social security taxes, Medicare taxes, and many other fees that many states refuse to call taxes. Secondly, it never occurred to them that as a society we do not pay a living wage. As illustrated in previous chapters, while CEOs salaries and other salaries have increased substantially, the average American salary has not.

It does not help when the senior tax policy analyst at the Heritage Foundation states that "We have 50 percent of people getting something for nothing". It is intellectually dishonest that he would characterize people that make too little to pay the income tax that way. Most Americans work. It is ironic that the same groups or organizations that attempt to demean those who make too little to pay income taxes do not see the dichotomy in their narrative when defending their support for tax breaks for corporations.

For those who have the false belief that it is somehow unjust that the more wealthy should have a larger tax burden, they must understand that the inordinate exponential increase in wealth by the very wealthy has nothing to do with their increase productivity, or more work but from the flawed design of our economic system that rewards the movement and appreciation of capital more so than an honest day's work, productivity, or innovation. In other words, if one inherits 100 million dollars one will never have to work, innovate, or provide anything to society on the march to billionaire status. Such a system is mathematically unsustainable.

Warren Buffet, the third richest person in the world speaking at a Hillary Clinton fundraiser in 2007 stated that he made forty six million dollars in income in 2006 (do not confuse income with wealth. At that time he was worth north of 52 billion dollars). He said he paid 17.7 per cent in income tax without attempting to find tax shelters to lessen the tax burden. His secretary who earned sixty thousand dollars was taxed at the higher rate of 30 per cent. Mr. Buffet went on to say that it was United States government policy that accentuated the disparity in wealth that hurt the economy by stifling opportunity and motivation.

If you bought 1000 shares of ACME stock at 100 dollars a share, a $100,000 investment. If that stock doubled in price (investment is now worth $200,000), the maximum amount of taxes you will pay on the $100,000 profit you made (capital gain) is 15% or $15,000. If you did an honest day's work and made $100,000 your marginal tax rate is 28%. Your ultimate tax bill would be $19,091. But that is not all, as an employee, you must pay 6.2% in social security taxes and 1.45% in Medicare taxes bringing your total tax liability to $26,741.00 ($19,091 Income Tax + $6,200 Social Security Tax + $1,450.00 Medicare Tax).

The disparity in how one's money is taxed allows for those who are wealthy to increasingly accumulate ever increasing wealth at a faster rate than a working person. Why; because "income" from capital appreciation (that increase in stock value) is taxed at a much lesser rate than income from work. As such the investing person (likely the wealthier person) has more disposable income to reinvest than the working person. That is a formula that is not easily overcome.

Contrary to popular belief our tax system is engineered to keep the average worker always at a financial disadvantage to the investor. In other words our tax policy rewards those that move and manipulate capital over those who would do an honest day's work.

It is not at all difficult to understand this reality; however with a Right Wing echo chamber that is good at conflating mutually exclusive issues, they have been able to convince a substantial number of Americans that the equitable taxing of wealth and the wealthy would be detrimental to our economy. Many Americans are likely willing to believe the fallacy because they naïvely believe that the American dream of anyone having equal opportunity to make it applies to them. Unfortunately under our current implementation of capitalism, the tenet that everyone has the same opportunity is nothing but a pipe dream.

If you are born poor in a poor neighborhood, you likely will attend an underfunded public school with substandard resources. A substandard education in one's formative years is a high mountain to climb that most simply do not even attempt.

The false belief that taxing the wealthy a bit more stifles economic growth is intellectually dishonest and was categorically disproved by the Clinton Administration's modest tax increases in the 1990s that led to a balanced budget, large increase in employment, decrease in poverty, and an all-around robust economy. Economic activity is determined by the speed and amount of money being spent. Tax breaks for the wealthy does not guarantee that taxes not paid would be spent or effectively invested. Taxes collected by the government are always spent thus generating demand and investment from said increased economic activity. That is the difference between trickle up and trickledown economics. Trickledown economics hopes the wealthy will allow some of their bounty to reach the masses while trickle up economics allows the masses to create a democratic demand.

Something extraordinary occurred on Sunday August 1st, 2010. Three prominent Americans versed in economics from all sides came out in support of letting the Bush Jr. Tax cuts expire for fiscally responsible reasons.

Alan Greenspan, previous Federal Reserve Chairman and free market conservative went on NBC's Meet The Press and told David Gregory that he does not support tax-cuts with borrowed money. Additionally he stated that unlike what most Republicans say, tax-cuts do not pay for themselves. [19] Greenspan seem to be recanting on some of his fundamental absolute market beliefs since our economy cratered. While the fortunes of those whose errors caused the catastrophic failure of our economy are functionally intact, average Americans are left to fend for themselves.

Fareed Zakaria, a Centrist, author, commentator, and political expert said the following

> *"We have to be willing to pay for the government we want, which by the way is among the smallest in the industrialized world.... Or we have to dramatically cut the government, which means cutting popular middle-class programs, since that's where the money is... So I have a proposal.... Let's let the entire slew of Bush Jr. tax cuts retire... That would take us back to Clinton-era rates, when the American economy had its strongest growth*

---

[19] Transcript at: http://bit.ly/bTKZ1M

years in three decades and the budget was balanced for the first time in four decades. "[20]

Fareed's statement is self-evident and obvious. Politicians with the help of focus groups to measure the psychology of their constituency are able to create appealing however invalid talking points that resonate. Of course they are assisted by lobbyist driven indoctrinating misleading advertising that subliminally influence these same citizens.

A classic example is the standard talking point used by those in favor of keeping the Bush Jr. tax cuts. They claim that it would hurt employment because small businessmen would be hit because they make more than $250,000. Of course they do not state that less than 2% of businesses have taxable incomes in excess of $250,000.

David Stockman, a staunch Conservative and President Reagan's OMB director & architect of Reagan's tax cut and supply-side economic policies came out with a striking article in the New York Times titled "Four

---

[20] Transcript at: http://bit.ly/aXKPAw.

Deformations of the Apocalypse" in which he rightfully illustrated the transformation of the Conservative fiscally responsible Republican leaders into nothing but "a mockery of traditional party ideals". He stated that:

> *"IF there were such a thing as Chapter 11 for politicians, the Republican push to extend the unaffordable Bush Jr. tax cuts would amount to a bankruptcy filing."*

> *"This debt explosion has resulted not from big spending by the Democrats, but instead the Republican Party's embrace, about three decades ago, of the insidious doctrine that deficits don't matter if they result from tax cuts"* (1)

On August 4th, 2010 Treasury Secretary Timothy Geithner gave a fiscal policy speech at The Center for American Progress where he further refuted many of the myths about the effect of letting tax cuts to the wealthy expire. Additionally he stated[21]

> *"[T]he policies put in place by the previous administration, prior to this great recession,*

---

[21] Full Webcast can be found at http://bit.ly/cfNZ98

have left us with a terrible legacy of challenges,"

"And America is a less equal country today than it was ten years ago, in part because of the tax cuts for the top 2 percent put in place in 2001 and 2003."

"We live in one of the richest economies in the world," the Treasury Secretary continued. "But one in eight Americans is on food stamps today."

"Fiscal discipline requires hard choices and we must be prepared to make them," he said. "[T]here is no credible argument to be made that the purpose of government is to borrow from future generations of Americans to finance an extension of tax cuts for the top 2 percent." (5)

Republicans now claim that via their young star US Representative Paul Ryan they have a new plan called "Roadmap for America's Future". This new plan is really continued tax cuts for the wealthy and draconian cuts for the middleclass.

On August 5th, 2010 Nobel Prize Winning Economist Paul Krugman dissected the plan illustrating the fraud that it really is. Pertinent excerpts from Krugman's article:

> *Mr. Ryan has become the Republican Party's poster child for new ideas thanks to his "Roadmap for America's Future," a plan for a major overhaul of federal spending and taxes. News media coverage has been overwhelmingly favorable; on Monday, The Washington Post put a glowing profile of Mr. Ryan on its front page, portraying him as the G.O.P.'s fiscal conscience. He's often described with phrases like "intellectually audacious."*

> *But it's the audacity of dopes. Mr. Ryan isn't offering fresh food for thought; he's serving up leftovers from the 1990s, drenched in flimflam sauce.*

> *Mr. Ryan's plan calls for steep cuts in both spending and taxes. He'd have you believe that the combined effect would be much lower budget deficits, and, according to that Washington Post report, he speaks about*

deficits "in apocalyptic terms." And The Post also tells us that his plan would, indeed, sharply reduce the flow of red ink: "The Congressional Budget Office has estimated that Rep. Paul Ryan's plan would cut the budget deficit in half by 2020."

But the budget office has done no such thing. At Mr. Ryan's request, it produced an estimate of the budget effects of his proposed spending cuts — period. It didn't address the revenue losses from his tax cuts.

The nonpartisan Tax Policy Center has, however, stepped into the breach. Its numbers indicate that the Ryan plan would reduce revenue by almost $4 trillion over the next decade. If you add these revenue losses to the numbers The Post cites, you get a much larger deficit in 2020, roughly $1.3 trillion.

And that's about the same as the budget office's estimate of the 2020 deficit under the Obama administration's plans. That is, Mr. Ryan may speak about the deficit in apocalyptic terms, but even if you believe that his proposed *spending cuts are feasible — which you shouldn't — the Roadmap wouldn't reduce the deficit. All it would do is cut benefits for the middle class while slashing taxes on the rich.*

And I do mean slash. The Tax Policy Center[22] finds that the Ryan plan would cut taxes on the richest 1 percent of the population in half, giving them 117 percent of the plan's total tax cuts. That's not a misprint. Even as it slashed taxes at the top, the plan would raise taxes for 95 percent of the population. (6)

What is disturbing is that serious mainstream media Liberal or Conservative coverage of these stories have been all but non-existent. No in-depth analysis as to why in the heat of the Bush Jr. tax-cut expiration debate would these prominent commentators, two of which are Conservative ideologues, so vocally and outwardly express their opinions to have the tax-cut expire in no uncertain terms. No in-depth analysis on Representative Paul Ryan's "Roadmap for America's Future" is performed by the mainstream media so that

---

[22] In-depth analysis of Paul Ryan's "Roadmap for America's Future" by the Tax Policy Center (http://bit.ly/aWHddc)

Americans can see the real price of Conservative policies.

One can only hope that more prominent economists and business leaders will come forward to provide cover to the few additional politicians that know they must make the tough choice for the country. The country is at a tipping point of being either Rome or remaining the USA.

Patent Law

The corruption of the Patent Law by corporations presents another example of why our brand of Capitalism is a failure. As long as corporations can use patent laws to stifle competition or force the use of their patents for fear of prosecution, the semblance of America being a free market is a wishful mental fabrication.

Amazon.com filed for a patent in 1997 on the procedure for placing an online order over the Internet. The procedure using the OneClick button used on the Amazon.com site was patented. This is tantamount to BestBuy patenting how a customer presents their credit card for payment for their products in some select way. The patent was ultimately granted. At the time I was contemplating creating a web based ordering software package but because of the potential legal issues I may have to go through after investing substantial development time, I decided to scrap the project. This has probably occurred thousands of times. It inhibits healthy competition and total societal progress from the inability of having many different sources developing similar products and services which ultimate reduces cost and makes for better products and services.

Farmers are one of the pillars of our society. America's farmers are productive because they work hard and because we have great universities that research best farming practices. America's farmers are also very productive because of the work of many scientists at major agri-businesses developing plant strains and genetically engineered plants and seeds.

Corporations are allowed to patent genes. The requirements to get said patents are not even very stringent.

> **Patenting Genes, Gene Fragments, SNPS, Gene Tests, Proteins, and Stem Cells** [23]
>
> **In terms of genetics**, *inventors must*
> *(1) identify novel genetic sequences,*
> *(2) specify the sequence's product,*
> *(3) specify how the product functions in nature --ie, its use*
> *(4) enable one skilled in the field to use the sequence for its stated purpose*

In creating genetically modified plants and patenting them corporations have claimed ownership to any seeds of these plants. This means that farmers that

---

[23] Genetics and Patenting: http://bit.ly/aGCNOo

want to grow these plants are obligated to purchase these seeds from the corporation owning the patent to these plants. If a farmer grows genetically modified soybeans or corn, they are prohibited from saving any of the seeds to plant for the next season. They are forced to purchase it from the corporation owning the patent on said seed.

Corporations vigorously prosecute farmers who they believe are keeping some of their own seeds. What is interesting is that the field of a farmer who is using genetically modified seeds adjacent to a farmer who is not using genetically modified seeds could be contaminated by cross pollination of the fields. This could result in the farmer not using genetically modified seed crops yield genetically modified seeds which could force him at great cost to prove that he was not farming with stolen seeds.

This is not hypothetical. Corporations vigorously go after farmers who they suspect are using genetically modified seeds they collect from their own fields. As of October 26th, 2007 Monsanto, a corporation owning the patent to Roundup ready soybeans, filed 112 lawsuits affecting 372 farmers and 49 small farm businesses[24]. Many of the farmers' fields were likely contaminated by adjacent users of Monsanto's genetically modified seeds. It is impossible for the farmer to definitively show that these seeds were not pirated yet legal costs could eventually make it necessary for farmers to just settle and purchase seeds from these corporations to prevent going out of business altogether. Allowing the patenting of genetically modified seeds sets a dangerous precedence. It is the doorway of corporate control of our food supply with any restriction said corporation may want to apply.

The U.S. Patent and Trademark Office have granted thousands of patents on human genes and about 20% of human genes are patented[25]. Any corporation owning a patent on any gene can prevent anyone from studying, viewing, or testing that gene. This undoubtedly inhibits the timely development of cures, drugs, medicines, or tests for fear of lawsuits from companies owning patents to the gene. Giving corporations or anyone or entity the ability to own patents on genes can only be considered obscene and

---

[24] Center For Food Safety: http://bit.ly/bMS4QO
[25] ACLU: http://bit.ly/bUhiA8

immoral. In our form of capitalism it is a method to ensure that those who have the capital to control genes and in that respect life will command unlimited profit.

On May 12, 2009, the ACLU and the Public Patent Foundation filed a lawsuit against Myriad Genetics and the University of Utah Research Foundation who hold patents on the genes BRCA1 and BRCA2 charging that patenting human genes violate the First Amendment and patent law because genes are "products of nature" and therefore cannot be patented.

On March 29th, 2010 the patents were invalidated[26]. The decision stated

> *The resolution of these motions is based upon long recognized principles of molecular biology and genetics: DNA represents the physical embodiment of biological information, distinct in its essential characteristics from any other chemical found in nature. It is concluded that DNA's existence in an "isolated" form alters*

---

[26] ACLU: http://bit.ly/bwWqux

*neither this fundamental quality of DNA as it
exists in the body nor the information it
encodes. Therefore, the patents at issue
directed to "isolated DNA" containing
sequences found in nature are unsustainable as
a matter of law and are deemed unpatentable
subject matter under 35 U.S.C. § 101.*

The decision is likely to be appealed eventually to the
Supreme Court. It is for this reason that those sitting
on the Supreme Courts matter. A court with a Right
Wing tilt tends to be more corporatists in nature as
opposed to ruling with biased toward the individual.
The current makeup of the Supreme Court has a Right
bias that unless a progressive president is maintained
will likely change said bias from a tilt to an absolute
Right Wing bend that is likely to further erode the
rights of the individual in favor of corporations.

There are many other examples one could use to
illustrate the destructive nature of patents. Ironically,
those who believe in the infallibility of the market
should really seek the abolishment of the patent as in
their parlance; the market would sort things out. Those
capable of bringing a product or service to bear at a
price and quality desired by customers would be

successful. The reality is the patent system is designed to allow a select few to control innovations in selected fields. Moreover it provides disincentives for the improvement of technologies for fear of patent infringement.

Military Spending

The following is an excerpt from President Dwight Eisenhower's 1961 farewell speech discussing the perils of the military industrial complex. Its relevance today is ever so present.

A vital element in keeping the peace is our military establishment. Our arms must be mighty, ready for instant action, so that no potential aggressor may be tempted to risk his own destruction.

Our military organization today bears little relation to that known by any of my predecessors in peacetime, or indeed by the fighting men of World War II or Korea.

Until the latest of our world conflicts, the United States had no armaments industry. American makers of plowshares could, with time and as required, make swords as well. But now we can no longer risk emergency improvisation of national defense; we have been compelled to create a permanent armaments industry of vast proportions. Added to this, three and a half million men and women are directly engaged in the defense establishment. We annually spend on military security more than the net income of all United States corporations.

This conjunction of an immense military establishment and a large arms industry is new in the American experience. The total influence -- economic, political, even spiritual -- is felt in every city, every State house, every office of the Federal government. We recognize the imperative need for this development. Yet we must not fail to comprehend its grave implications. Our toil, resources and livelihood are all involved; so is the very structure of our society.

In the councils of government, we must guard against the acquisition of unwarranted influence, whether sought or unsought, by the military industrial complex. The potential for the disastrous rise of misplaced power exists and will persist.

We must never let the weight of this combination endanger our liberties or democratic processes. We should take nothing for granted. Only an alert and knowledgeable

*citizenry can compel the proper meshing of the
huge industrial and military machinery of
defense with our peaceful methods and goals,
so that security and liberty may prosper
together.*

These words were not heeded. While we have by far
the largest and most sophisticated military, this comes
at the expense of keeping our country's infrastructure
state of the art and many other investments including
education, alternative energy, environmental cleanup
and much more.

The following chart details the huge disparity in our
country's military spending relative to the rest of the
world. It is completely disproportionate that the
country closest to us in military expenditure, China,
spends eight times less than we do.

2008 Defense Expenditure (in billions of current U.S. dollars)[27]

Country	2008 Spending
United States (including war and nuclear)	696.3
Rest of NATO	325.5
Non-NATO Europe	26.8
Russia	86.0
Middle East and North Africa	110.5
Sub-Saharan Africa	12.1
South and Central Asia	41.2
East Asia and Australasia	131.3
China	83.5
Latin America and Caribbean	58.0

In effect the United States citizens have been indoctrinated into believing that we must be the police, the enforcer, and the protector of the rest of the world. It is amazing that the same ideology that

---

[27] The Center For Arms Control And Non-Proliferation.

has little sympathy for the disenfranchised or the poor, claiming that providing assistance makes them less likely to care for themselves, do not support that tenet where our military spending is concerned. The hypocrisy is that most of the spending is nothing but a method of keeping an industry propped up with cash and a covert form of transferring taxpayer wealth to the stockholders of the military industrial complex, the multitude of corporations specializing in the defense industry.

On May 3rd, 2010, Secretary of Defense Robert M Gates gave a speech[28] at the Gaylord Convention Center, National Harbor, Maryland. The following telling excerpt details the magnitude of our excessive military hardware.

It is important to remember that, as much as the U.S. battle fleet has shrunk since the end of the Cold War, the rest of the world's navies have shrunk even more. So, in relative terms, the U.S. Navy is as strong as it has ever been.

In assessing risks and requirements even in light of an expanding array of global missions and responsibilities

---

[28] US Department of Defense (http://bit.ly/9dr18G)

– everything from shows of presence to humanitarian relief – some context is useful:

- *The U.S. operates 11 large carriers, all nuclear powered. In terms of size and striking power, no other country has even one comparable ship.*
- *The U.S. Navy has 10 large-deck amphibious ships that can operate as sea bases for helicopters and vertical-takeoff jets. No other navy has more than three, and all of those navies belong to pur allies or friends. Our Navy can carry twice as many aircraft at sea as all the rest of the world combined.*
- *The U.S. has 57 nuclear-powered attack and cruise missile submarines – again, more than the rest of the world combined.*
- *Seventy-nine Aegis-equipped combatants carry roughly 8,000 vertical-launch missile cells. In terms of total missile firepower, the U.S. arguably outmatches the next 20 largest navies.*
- *All told, the displacement of the U.S. battle fleet – a proxy for overall fleet capabilities – exceeds, by one recent estimate, at least the next 13 navies combined, of which 11 are our allies or partners.*
- *And, at 202,000 strong, the Marine Corps is the largest military force of its kind in the world and exceeds the size of most world armies.*

In his speech he further details the insanity of other hardware potentially in the pipeline like twelve subs at seven billion dollars each. He details the fight with Congress to cease production of the C-17 cargo aircraft and an end to funding an extra engine for the Joint Strike Fighter even though the military proper supports this.

Free Trade

Politicians have touted free trade as a policy that would increase our employment & increase demand for American products. This is another case of corporations attempting to convince Americans to support policies that simply are not in their own best interest and in fact has and will continue to have a material negative effect on middle class America. Free trade is another policy that ultimately results in the transfer of wealth from the middle class to other countries and to the stockholders of corporations who choose to manufacture overseas. Free trade is a conduit for outsourcing on steroids.

Manufacturing in America is much more costly than manufacturing in countries like China, India, or Vietnam. Their manufacturing costs are lower for multiple reasons.

- Their unit labor cost is much less than ours as they have a virtually unlimited labor pool of poor people willing to work for pennies on the dollar relative to an American worker.
- Their industries do not have strict environmental restrictions.

- They are not saddled with the type of healthcare cost our industry is saddled with for a lack of a real universal healthcare system.

All humans trained or educated for a particular job or task whether in the United States, China, Vietnam, Costa Rica, Panamá, or any other country will perform a particular job effectively. Any country that offers the lowest cost to corporations for producing a product or service will likely cause said corporation to move its manufacturing or service to the lower cost country. This is not conjecture but reality in just about every industry in the United States.

I own a small software company that develops custom software. I receive calls weekly from Indian corporations that offer software design and development for $10.00 per hour. The average software engineer's salary in the US is about $65,000 per year ($31.25 per hour). These $10.00 per hour Indian engineers are just as competent as American engineers.

It is not only software developer/engineers being outsourced. There is ample advertising by foreign corporations to US corporations for outsourcing their radiologists. I found this narrative on one of the Indian websites advertising to our corporations for outsourcing various medical services performed by medical professionals including radiologists.

Pricing Advantages

Our pricing will save you more than 60% of the cost of conducting your medical billing or coding practices onshore.

Another significant advantage of outsourcing Healthcare services lies in space utilization, especially in places with high real estate value. Medical billing, coding and transcription services involve data entry and processing functions, which require a large workforce. This workforce will take up substantial space in your office premises. Outsourcing such functions will enable this space to be used for other core business functions- a smarter use of precious real estate[29].

While the narrative may be appealing to the shareholder of the hospital, it is the seed of marginalization of more American jobs and the local care of patients.

---

[29] Outsource2india (http://bit.ly/cWvGZP)

The American textile industry has been decimated. The vast majority of our clothes are made elsewhere. Between 1997 to the present over 1298 textile mills have been closed according to NCTO with most of these closings in North Carolina, South Carolina, Georgia, and Virginia. It is estimated that 39.4 % of the industry's jobs were lost[30].

The auto industry has been hit hard as well by outsourcing. Even though many cars are made in America, ironically many parts and spare parts are outsourced to China and many other countries. In the process we lose the expertise of casters, lathe operators, and many other machinist and trades people. Can we really build anything solely with American expertise anymore?

The loss of many jobs and industries to outsourcing is a danger to our country. At first it was mostly blue collar manufacturing jobs that were exported. With the advent of the Internet and the ubiquity of real time communication it affords, professionals are now finding that their jobs are now being outsourced.

---

[30] The National Council of Textile Organizations (NCTO) (http://bit.ly/d7VUv0) provided excellent information on mill closures and job losses.

Software Engineers, Medical Doctors, and just about any other professional is now a candidate for outsourcing.

As jobs are outsourced there is little incentive for people to get into a heavily outsourced field. This creates a national vacuum for that skill set as it is lost for however long that skill set is required to master. As an example, if the radiology field becomes heavily outsourced, it is unlikely that anyone would find it worthwhile to get an expensive education in radiology giving that employment would be scarce or the pay low.

To be clear, we need trade. We need fair trade not free trade. We also need our country to ensure that the population maintains all skills to be self-sufficient. If we lose our ability to create machined goods we are dependent on a foreign power. This applies to all skill sets. This is a national security issue that should be addressed.

Government Social Services

The civilized are those who have constructed an effective government that governs under the premise that we can have a more secure and humane existence collectively than by ourselves. The founders of our country created our governing document, the Constitution, that while not perfect was designed with the ability to change as we became more enlightened or as realities changed. Many on the Right wrap themselves in the constitution as a premise for maintaining the status quo. Their view of the constitution as a template that should be strictly interpreted literally as opposed to a living document that should be interpreted in a manner relevant to our current realities is simply wrong.

Had the founding fathers been infallible in their humanity we would not have needed the 14th amendment that codified blacks as full citizens, the 19th amendment that gave women the right to vote, or the 24th amendment that prevented state restrictions on voters. The constitution was written in the 18th century. It would simply be naïve to believe that our founding fathers could envision today's technology, today's demographics, or today's international reality.

Not allowing evolvement inhibits our country's progress.

While some bathe themselves in the supremacy of the constitution as if it is an infallible document, those aggrieved by it cannot consider it as such. Moreover given that it reflected those who wrote it, its flaws are inherently the flaws of its authors, the founding fathers. While I give them their due for ultimately creating a document with the semblance of democracy, it was but a building block needing modification to make it live up to the excellent preamble

> *We the People of the United States, in Order to form a more perfect Union, establish Justice, insure domestic Tranquility, provide for the common defense, promote the general Welfare, and secure the Blessings of Liberty to ourselves and our Posterity, do ordain and establish this Constitution for the United States of America.*

For many that only became true with a lot of work, blood, tears, and sacrifice. The premise is that the purpose of this constitution, the reason for its being, the reason for its existence among other things is to

"promote the general Welfare". In that light there are basic governmental services that are required to ensure the promotion of the general welfare.

No one can argue that the establishment of social security does not promote the general welfare, insure domestic tranquility, or secure the Blessings of Liberty to ourselves and our posterity. After-all, social security provides millions of hard working Americans, many who had not made a real living wage the ability to simply survive on a subsistence level, but survive. Moreover, one could argue that it insures Domestic Tranquility as a population in dire need ultimately revolts.

No one can argue that in an economic system based on free enterprise that at any given time any American can be unemployed. Moreover, no one can argue that children should ever have to go hungry, uneducated, or homeless because of the unemployment or underemployment of their parents whether by a bad economy or by irresponsibility. Responsible welfare programs designed to prevent program abuse makes society humane.

The reality is while many on the Right imply that welfare abuse is rampant, that is far from true. If this concern were genuine, their concern would extend to corporate welfare.

Where is the concern for inflated prices we pay private contractors for feeding our troops in Iraq and Afghanistan? It is much less expensive to have military personnel cook and feed its own than to hire a company who does that specific job for a profit. The cost per plate of food in Iraq is more expensive than most high end restaurants in the US. Is that corporate welfare? Of course it is.

Where was the concern when banks were providing student loans at high interest rates while the government assumed all the risk for defaults on these loans? The Student Loan program was one of the biggest frauds on the American taxpayer. In addition to paying fees to banks, in effect the American Government became the insurance company for the bank if any student defaulted on their student loans. The Obama administration passed a bill that instead lends directly to students. As reported in The New York Times

The new law will eliminate fees paid to private banks to act as intermediaries in providing loans to college students and use much of the nearly $68 billion in savings over 11 years to expand Pell grants and make it easier for students to repay outstanding loans after graduating. The law also invests $2 billion in community colleges over the next four years to provide education and career training programs to workers eligible for trade adjustment aid after dislocation in their industries.

The law will increase Pell grants along with inflation in the next few years, which should raise the maximum grant to $5,975 from $5,550 by 2017, according to the White House, and it will also provide 820,000 more grants by 2020. (6)

There is no purpose other than corporate welfare for having the government student loan program run through private banks. The Right Wing of course accused the Obama administration of socializing lending. They claim government lending to American students is socialization while giving welfare to businesses for no value added service or risk, capitalism.

Where was the concern for Medicare Advantage, privately run Medicare which provides no better results than government run Medicare but siphons profits? Selective concern is intellectually disingenuous.

No one can argue that Medicare does not provide for the well-being of our older citizens. Yet, those on the Right fought it as being socialism, communism, and every implied negative "ism" in between. In fact in 1961 the Right's Messiah, Ronald Reagan pushed the propaganda[31], the fallacy that the passage of Medicare would lead us to socialism. Today our seniors can be assured that irrespective of their socio-economic condition, they will get the healthcare they need. Ironically the same arguments that were made during the Medicare debate were simply dusted off and reused to scare the wits out of Americans during the Healthcare Reform Debate.

---

[31] The entire recording can be listened to on YouTube at http://youtu.be/AYrlDlrLDSQ

That the constitution did not codify the government to create Universal Healthcare does not prohibit it from doing so. Just as Social Security and Medicare are constitutional, so is the ability of the government to implement Universal Healthcare.

Many during the healthcare debate have been victims to the same type of propaganda used by the Oligarchy in third world countries to maintain policies that hurt the very same citizens who would benefit from the change in our policy. Third world Oligarchs create sideshows having nothing to do with the issue, outright lie, or simply deceive people by stoking their most carnal insecurities and prejudices; henceforth, the tone that was the healthcare debate.

The great healthcare deception followed a proven formula.

- Create a visceral hate of anything having to do with the government by inflating its failures and ignoring its successes. Of course no balance is given to how things were before government involvement.
- Inflate the successes of the specific institution controlled by the Oligarchy and ignore its

failures e.g., lack of regulation that caused the oil spill disaster in the Gulf of Mexico causing the immediate death of 11, likely thousands from oil exposure related illnesses, and the permanent destruction of the livelihood of thousands.

- Associate anyone or entity promoting any government involvement as a communist, socialist, un-American that want to take away your freedom.
- Associate our founding with unabated free market laissez faire capitalism.

Because of how little citizens read and learn independent of talk radio and television, this type of indoctrination is very effective. If we are unable or unwilling to work on educating ourselves objectively we will continue our decline into third world status. This template almost derailed any substantive healthcare reform from being passed.

Anyone with private insurance should read their policy. Every private insurance company controls every aspect of your healthcare. They control which doctors will get paid, which hospitals you can use, which medicines will be allowed. Moreover they always reserve the right to cancel, rescind, or deny your coverage. Most people do not realize this until they most need it.

Rescission is one of the most obscene insurance companies' practices in which insurance companies collect premiums for months, years, or decades. When the patient is subsequently diagnosed with some expensive covered illness, they navigate their database to find some error the patient made when they originally applied for insurance. If it is found, they cancel the insurance policy, do not return paid premiums, and do not pay the patients' healthcare costs. It was instructive during the healthcare debate to watch the insurance executives at a Healthcare Reform Congressional Hearing[32] attempt to explain the criteria for their rescissions. Some had in excess of two thousand criteria that could cause a rescission. What was telling was when Congressman Stupak asked the insurance companies if they would commit to not rescind anyone's policies if they did not fraudulently mislead in their insurance application. They all said to the utter disregard of humanity that they would not. Inasmuch as these insurance executives were trying to

---

[32] The illustrative part of the hearing can be found at http://youtu.be/Y97__KA4xHQ.

convince Congress that a system with private insurance was preferred, the reasons they should not exist in a humane healthcare system was there for everyone to see.

One must read the entire Healthcare Reform Bill[33]. No one requires an arbiter of the insurance companies to interpret the bill. Many of the excerpts of the bill emailed by many Congress people to their constituents were simply shameful lies or misrepresentations of specifics in the bill. We should all be for free speech but it should not guarantee the right to misinform especially from those who govern.

The mainstream media displayed a degree of incompetence that superseded the incompetence we saw during the lead up to the war in Iraq. Just like it took the Bush Jr. administration by its word on the fallacies that caused us to invade Iraq, it took insurance company and other corporatist cohorts assertions at face value. Moreover, when Republicans blatantly lied about items in the Healthcare Reform Bill, the mainstream media never challenged them

---

[33] Easily understood specifics of the Healthcare Reform Bill, how it affects you, how to use it for your healthcare can be found at http://www.healthcare.gov.

forcefully but accepted their assertions as a valid part of the discussion. The Iraq war media blunder is partially excusable since much information was classified. The Healthcare Reform Debate coverage blunder is not, as all relevant information is readily available.

The reality is the Healthcare Reform bill is mostly a Republican bill that is now opposed by those who proposed its major tenets. The individual mandate was proposed early on by Senator McCain, Tommy Thompson, & Mitt Romney. The disingenuous "death panels" which really allow the payment for responsible counsel for end of life care was supported in 2008 by Sarah Palin, Newt Gingrich, Senator Grassley, and many others since the Bush Jr. administration. This hypocrisy was debunked by Think Progress[34] who wrote:

> *However, on April 16th 2008, then Gov. Sarah Palin endorsed some of the same end of life counseling she now decries as a form of euthanasia. In a proclamation announcing "Healthcare Decisions Day," Palin urged*

---

[34] Think Progress: For 'Death Panels' Before She Was Against Them? Palin Endorsed End Of Life Counseling As Governor (http://bit.ly/9rDTEa)

*public facilities to provide better information
about advance directives, and made it clear that
it is critical for seniors to be informed of such
options:*

*WHEREAS, Healthcare Decisions Day is
designed to **raise public awareness of the need
to plan ahead for healthcare decisions, related
to end of life care** and medical decision-making
whenever patients are unable to speak for
themselves and to **encourage the specific use of
advance directives to communicate these
important healthcare decisions.** [...]*

*WHEREAS, one of the principal goals of
Healthcare Decisions Day is to **encourage
hospitals, nursing homes, assisted living
facilities, continuing care retirement
communities, and hospices to participate in a
statewide effort to provide clear and consistent
information** to the public about advance
directives, as well as to **encourage medical
professionals and lawyers to volunteer their
time and efforts to improve public knowledge
and increase the number of Alaska's citizens
with advance directives.***

*WHEREAS, the Foundation for End of Life Care
in Juneau, Alaska, and other organizations
throughout the United States have endorsed this*

event and are committed to educating the public about the importance of discussing healthcare choices and executing advance directives.

Though this proclamation is now deleted from the Alaska governor's website, it shows that Palin's current fear-mongering is purely political. Palin is not the only conservative leader completely flip-flopping on this issue. Merely months ago, Gingrich too endorsed end of life counseling. At a conference in April of this year, Gingrich said advance directives can "save money" while also helping to "decrease the stress felt by caregivers."

This pattern of disingenuous objections repeats itself over and over. Unfortunately we have a press whose research departments seem devoid of research and a significant part of the population that is willing to accept FoxNews, Rush Limbaugh, Glenn Beck, & Sean Hannity as legitimate sources of information irrespective of their daily barrage of easily disproved misinformation. What makes this ever so sad is that just about every speech, live or written by politicians is available all over the Internet.

During the Healthcare Reform debate I randomly called 50 telephone numbers throughout Canada, a country with a universal healthcare system. The Canadian system was demonized by many on the Right. Not one of the 50 Canadians I called would opt-out of their system. Ironically many took offense to the falsehoods that were found in the ads by those opposing reform. This is clearly understood when the following facts are taken into account.

US / Canada Comparisons[35]

Fact:
US Healthcare as % of GDP: 15.3%
Canada Healthcare as % of GDP: 10%

Fact:
US Per Capita Cost of Healthcare: $6714.00
Canada Per Capita Cost of Healthcare: $3,678.00

Fact:
Government Spending on Healthcare Per Capita is 23% higher in the US than Canada.

---

[35] Cost of Administering Healthcare in US Vs Canada Vs All Countries
The New England Journal Of Medicine (http://bit.ly/9saDTa)
OECD Health Data 2009 (http://bit.ly/ct2Qly)
World Health Organization (http://bit.ly/bzWllr)

Fact:
Canadian health outcomes are better than ours.

Basic Statistics	U.S.	Canada
Life Expectancy (Male)	74.8	77.4
Life Expectancy (Female)	80.1	82.4
Infant Mortality/1000 live births	6.8	5.3
Obesity Rate (Male)	31.1	17.0
Obesity Rate (Female)	32.2	19.0
HC spending as % of GDP (2005)	16.0%	10.4%

A healthcare system void of profits is a healthcare system that would not be innovative. One should first determine which part of our healthcare industry is innovative. Non-ideological thinking would immediately discern that insurance companies' services are simply the equivalent of paying a bill for a profit, attempting to maximize their profits to shareholders and executives. While many will claim that insurance companies in addition to paying a bill handles risk management and negotiates reduced costs for services, their ultimate and legitimate goal is not the interest of the patient but the shareholder. The only way to accomplish this is to deny services to their clients, rescind insurance policies where possible, and form incestuous relationships with specific doctors, hospitals, and drug companies thus eliminating the insured the choice to their respective doctors or procedures.

While the development of drugs, the development of medical devices, the development of more patient friendly and efficient hospitals, and hospital procedures inherently benefit from a profit motive and should maintain a for profit component, insurance companies provide nothing to the equation other than to create an entity that skims in excess of 30% of our healthcare dollars which could be more effectively used to provide additional healthcare to many. Not even the vilified government with all its waste is that inefficient.

While it is easy to demonize the government, one must take responsibility for the government we elect. Moreover the false belief that somehow the government is inherently less trustworthy than private enterprise in the free market is nothing more than an ideological fallacy. The reality is that we need them both. After all the corruptions we so blame the government for, are nothing more than private enterprise being said corrupting agent of government. In privatizing wars we the government pay a private company soldier more than our regular soldiers for the same job. The government pays private health insurance companies to pay Medicare bills at a profit that they could pay themselves.

Anyone who believes that we can solve our healthcare problems solely by opening up interstate competition, providing subsidies to the uninsured, eliminating caps, and allowing high risk pools for those with pre-existing conditions misses the entire cost savings within the entire healthcare reform bill. These alone provides little incentive for cost savings as the structural 30% cost of private health insurance company overhead remains as well as redundant practices in the industry at large. Moreover the fact that a high risk pool would be created to differentiate those with pre-existing conditions unfairly penalizes the sick.

Healthcare reform was a must. Universal healthcare and social security are rights that are consistent with our Constitution where it states "promote the general welfare". While the Healthcare Reform Bill that passed was built on the private insurance model with no government provided insurance option to keep private insurance in check, increasing cost by the ever increasing need for growth by insurance companies will likely lead to this issue being revisited to reduce cost. Ironically the insurance companies that claimed they are more efficient than government balked at having American citizens have the choice of government run insurance versus a private insurance.

No one wants a government takeover of healthcare, however private health insurance have failed because the current model is not sustainable. Unregulated free markets do not understand humanity and with profit maximization being the guide for most executives, our manufacturing sectors have disaffected millions and our healthcare system continues a journey of inhumanness.

We reward those who move money vis-à-vis insurance executive, bankers, and stockbrokers more so than our real engines of production, the people. We then collect less taxes to run our government from the wealthy and semi wealthy. Borrow from the wealthy and semi-wealthy via bonds, pay the wealthy and semi-wealthy a guaranteed fairly high interest on said bonds with tax payer dollars, and then complain about deficit spending for the inability to have comprehensive healthcare.

The country cannot survive as we've known with a minute upper class, small upper middle class, and large lower class and poor. We could not build enough Walmarts to support that model. The migration of the masses to the bottom will continue while the very small upper and upper middle classes continue to flourish on outsourcing and wealth transfer.

President Obama was correct in stating that bringing back our economy and bringing back America to fiscal responsibility begins with healthcare. Basic health determines your ability to work. Moreover healthcare cost is the portion of our national budget that is growing unsustainably.

Those who still oppose the Healthcare Reform Bill should note that the cost of the program simply bring honesty to our healthcare accounting. After all, those without insurance have always been able to get care however late at a much higher cost than those with health insurance. Ultimately indigent care has always been paid through higher insurance premiums, increased taxes, or deficit spending.

The Market

If you listen to CNBC or any business channel you would think the market, our supposedly free market system is God Almighty that has the solution to every problem. This market is supposed to be intelligent. This market automatically identifies societal needs. This market is the most efficient way to allocate capital. If shortages of some resource occur, the market will solve said shortage. This is hogwash. A market has as much intelligence as the titans of finance that cooperate with their god, the market.

Early on I described how an ideal business would come to fruition in a real free enterprise system. I also described the basic financial services needed by any business. Those requirements do not require a financial sector of the size we currently have which is on the order of 8% of our GDP. That segment of our economy is saturated with ultra-high wage earners that produce no product or real service in the economy.

This god, the market really does not understand humanity. The market understands nothing about science or engineering. This market understands nothing about loyalty to country. It is a monolith solely interested in the maximization of wealth irrespective of the damage to the human condition or environment.

The oil industry presents a classic case where they are in fact following current corrupt market principles to maximize their shareholder value. The following facts cannot be refuted:

- Shareholders of companies within the oil industries reap tremendous profits from importing relatively inexpensive oil. In the aggregate Americans purchase of oil from overseas while making a few wealthy, is large transfer of our country's wealth to countries that are neither intrinsically friendly to us nor democratic.

- One of the reasons our military budget is as large as it is and specifically why we support a navy as large as we have is to ensure largely the ability to assure that no one will attempt to close shipping lanes for the transport of oil. If being in Iraq did not play a strategic importance to our oil supply we would not have spent the trillion+ dollars we spent there. Moreover, we would not have put the brave American patriotic soldiers in wars where we are simply marking time to ensure a relatively constant flow of oil.

- We provide oil companies with subsidies like the depletion allowance and many others. Inasmuch as every American in some fashion is paying taxes to support our oversized military to support these companies, they continue to protest any type of responsible tax increases.

- The true cost of the oil we use does not take into consideration its effects on our environment. Illnesses caused by the processing of hydrocarbons, illnesses caused by the burning of hydrocarbons, climate change caused by the burning of hydrocarbons, and water table and soil contamination caused by hydrocarbons are not reflected in the cost of this resource.

- In 2007 oil prices were rising sharply as we were entering the most severe recession since the Great Depression. This was the market at work. Nothing illegal occurred.

The Right likes to constantly assert that capitalism supposedly presents the best way to allocate resources. Yet every time there is a downturn they come running to the government (the taxpayer) for assistance.

As of the writing of this book unemployment is at 9.5% and underemployment likely around 16%. Interesting enough there is no shortage of things that need to be done in our country.

- Our infrastructure needs rebuilding. Drive around any city or country road in the United States and one would see bridges in the state you would only expect in a third world country. One does not have to look but to the I-35 Bridge collapsing in Minnesota. This kind of thing is not supposed to happen in the number one country in the world. Many of our roads are in such state of disrepair that they damage our automobiles. With states losing tax revenues because of the unemployment and underemployment rate as well as the loss in property values, this is likely to get much worst.
- We need more teachers in the classroom. Teachers more than ever are needed for the change forthcoming for preparing current and future generations for the new professions and methodologies that will be needed in our

economy going forward. There is a lack of vision to realize that the teaching profession is one of the areas where we should be expanding. With all those out of work it is the time to retrain.

- Immediate and substantial investments in research and development in alternative energy sources is needed. While today's corrupt capitalist model dictates that we use cheap Middle East, South American, and Canadian oil, this is directly against our national interest. A country that uses the volume of oil we use does national harm to our balance of trade by importing that much energy. Capitalism does not understand national interest. It only understands the interest of the relatively few shareholders.

- We need to build out our energy infrastructure for today's technology. The power grid needs to be expanded to places where we can take advantage of local energy sources flushed with geo-thermal energy, wind energy, and solar energy. Again the avid capitalist sees this as a poor allocation of resources since tax payers will pay for a military to keep shipping lanes open and countries politically in check to allow the cheap extraction of resources and cheap shipping.

- We need to make the term Made in America a national security issue. The systematic exporting of our jobs because it makes financial sense for the profits of corporations is the illustrative example of how our implementation of capitalism is anti-American.

The Right in order to confuse will try to attack all those rightfully pointing out the defects in our capitalism as communists or socialists. They know that those words instill a Soviet era fear in the baby boomer and older generation. The reality is that America is a socialist state, more so for corporations than for the average citizen.

Social Security, Medicare, Medicaid, & now Healthcare Reform make citizens minimally socialist. Major corporations however are the biggest recipient of taxpayer dollars. Ever heard the term "privatizing profits and socializing loss"? This is our government's relationship with major corporations. It is for this reason that instead of nationalizing the banks we infused them with capital during this Great Recession.

Capitalism, specifically capital markets are supposed to be self-regulating. When the titans of finance destroyed our economy they all left with multi-million dollar bonuses, bonuses for failure. They fail they collect. They succeed they collect even more.

That we have a 10% unemployment with all the work that needs to be done in the country with the enumerated problems above, is proof positive of a failure of our brand of capitalism. Given that the private sector is unable to match this unbalance of work to those seeking work it is imperative that some alternative system provide the catalyst to do so. The only entity capable is the government.

This is where government must trump "the market" for the better good of the country. It must institute policies for the long term benefit of the country.

The Media

I often wonder how such a large percentage of educated Americans can be so

- Misinformed to the real genesis of our exploding debt which provably is a result of taxation not consummate with the average American desired level of government spending. Americans still believe incorrectly that just cutting pork (earmarks) and a few entitlements would make a substantial dent in our deficit

- Misinformed about our military being as large as it is. We spend more on our military than the sum of most countries in the world combined. In other words almost 50% of all military spending in the world is spent by the US tax payer.

- Misinformed to the real reasons why healthcare reform requires full participation, a mandate. Whether government forces everyone to buy insurance or not, it is the responsible citizens taking care of those who decide to be irresponsible by fiat. Unless we will deny those without health insurance healthcare it is dishonest not to require everyone to purchase health insurance. Ironically, the mandate that Republicans are objecting to and suing about now is a Republican idea previously supported by George Bush Sr., Chuck Grassley, and a myriad of other Republicans. Moreover, Healthcare Reform if implemented as codified is paid for and brings down the structural deficit.

- Misinformed in believing illegal aliens take more out of our society than they provide. Inasmuch as the borders must be secured, illegal aliens are being made scapegoats even as they played a major role in our long economic expansion. Major corporations and many business people hire illegal aliens knowingly. Those displaced by these companies instead blame the illegal immigrant. They do not hold the company accountable.

- Misinformed and indoctrinated that somehow a corporation whose primary allegiance is to the fiduciary responsibility of its owners/shareholders is somehow more trustworthy than a government that is duly elected by the people and can be fired every two, four, or six years. Corporations are not intrinsically evil; it is simply that unlike a government that must work for the betterment of the citizenry at large, a corporation's only duty is to maximize profits for its shareholders.

- Misinformed about our current economic system that by design concentrates the country's wealth in the hands of a few. While most would like to believe that a pathway is available for anyone to get ahead, for most it is but a dream. Why should a wealthy man drinking tea at his pool in his mansion watching his stock appreciate pay less taxes on said appreciation (capital gains when sold) while that guy that goes to work every day pays a higher rate of income tax as he makes more income. The reason is bogus but everyone buys that capital gains is somehow a different kind of money than income made by doing a hard day's work.

- Misinformed that governmental policy could make corporations' propensity to export jobs more painful and less profitable. Corporations have exported American jobs and will not bring back American jobs until their extortion in demanding low American wages is realized thus reducing the standard of living of the masses while transferring wealth from these savings to the wealthiest amongst us.

- Misinformed about the negative effect of labor unions. Businesses have the Chamber of Commerce that work in concert to maximize laws that benefit companies. Just about every sector in the economy has multiple organizations that lobby local and federal government to pass business friendly regulation. Unless workers are unionized they have no leverage for higher wages and benefits. Workers provide the medium by which shareholders and executives make their exorbitant profits and salaries, they should be compensated appropriately.

Why are so many Americans so misinformed? Americans are misinformed firstly because they do not get their information independently. Secondly, Americans have been programmed to believe everything emanating from the media. With a fractured and polarized media we get a fractured and polarized populace.

Unfortunately the Right Wing in this country has made a portion of the media not an objective arbiter of news but a propaganda arm of their ideology. As a propaganda arm, whose sole intent is to have government policies passed that benefit the top echelon of their constituency, it becomes necessary to obfuscate truth to create false outrage to either stifle policies they disagree with or get bad policies passed.

Case in point is healthcare reform. It is fact that private insurance companies inflated profits and manufactured overhead increase the cost of premiums for the individual as well as the government. As such it would be much more efficient for the government to become the insurance company of record where all premiums paid actually pay for healthcare. Currently having multiple health insurance companies mean each company must have an advertising budget to compete against each other. Each insurance company has an overpaid CEO, CFO, & President. Each insurance company has an accounting department, a human resourced department, property overhead, etc. When all these are factored in, up to 30% of insurance payments go towards expenses not related to healthcare. Interesting enough Medicare, the government run healthcare program maligned by the

Right Wing has just a 3% expense overhead. Inasmuch as the above is fact, those on the Right insisted on the fallacy that competition would magically still make private insurance more efficient and inexpensive.

The hypocrisy in the debate was astounding. As a compromise it was suggested that in addition to private insurance a government run insurance company (the public option) be among the choices that Americans could choose from. After all, if those on the Right are correct then all Americans would eventually migrate to private insurance. Of course Right Wing Republicans and Right Wing Democrats wanted no part of it. The reason why? The results would have proven that having the government be the health insurance company of record would immediately prove more efficient. A single payer system's efficiency mathematically could not be equaled. The Right Wing Republicans and Right Wing Democrats were simply wrong and were simply working on behalf of the insurance companies.

The Right Wing propaganda engine is well positioned. They have the radio saturated with the likes of Rush Limbaugh, Sean Hannity, Michael Savage, Mark Levin, Glenn Beck, and other minor hosts that repeat the same misinforming and lying talking points on cue. It is amazing how it seems they are all reading from the same script. What is disconcerting is that the most popular of these hosts have neither any formal extended education or self-education consummate with the policies they attempt to take a position on. In addition to radio saturation, the FoxNews channel has become the de facto media outlet of the Republican Party. It is not at all difficult to see why those who watch only FoxNews and listen to Right Wing talk radio are so misinformed. They live in an alternate reality because FoxNews have created their reality.

Case in point on how they manufacture news, spin the news for some gain, and through continuous repetition, make it a reality for its viewers can be shown with the following New Black Panther story. I expand on this particular inconsequential story because this type of misinforming news is dangerous.

FoxNews and talk radio are attempting to make white America somehow a victim of two thugs from an inconsequential group, The New Black Panther Party, by accusing the Obama administration of not prosecution them for a perceived voter intimidation charge. They attempt to stoke their most carnal insecurities and prejudices. From Media Matters

> *The Republican vice chairwoman of the U.S. Commission on Civil Rights, which is currently investigating the Justice Department's decision, has said that the case is "very small potatoes" and that it has been surrounded by "overheated rhetoric filled with insinuations and unsubstantiated charges." She has further stated that the investigation has not "served the interests of the Commission" and that the DOJ has given a "plausible argument" for not pursuing additional charges in the case.*

> *Media Matters reviewed Fox News' coverage of the phony New Black Panther Party scandal on America Live and Fox News' evening shows available in Nexis from June 30 through July 14:*

> - *America Live has discussed the phony scandal during 45 segments totaling more than 3.5 hours since Kelly's June 30 interview with Adams.*
> - *The O'Reilly Factor has discussed the phony scandal during 18 segments*

totaling more than 1 hour since Kelly's interview.

- *Glenn Beck has discussed the phony scandal during 15 segments totaling more than 2 hours since Kelly's interview.*
- *Hannity has discussed the phony scandal during 10 segments totaling more than 42 minutes since Kelly's interview.*
- *Special Report with Bret Baier has discussed the phony scandal during 6 segments totaling more than 14 minutes since Kelly's interview.*

On the Record with Greta Van Susteren has discussed the phony scandal during 1 segment totaling more than 7 minutes since Kelly's interview. (6)

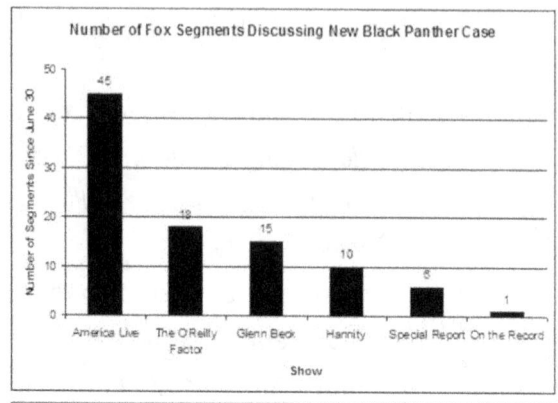

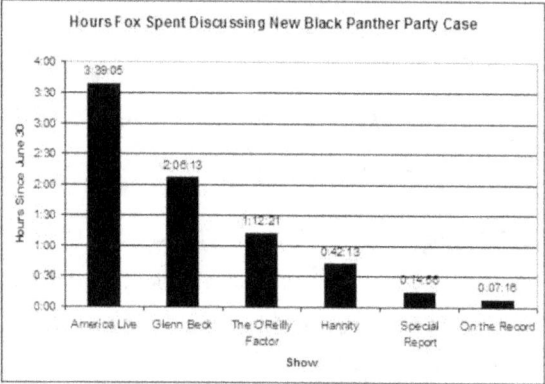

The above illustrates how FoxNews creates an alternate reality; saturation of misinformation that gives fallacy the semblance of truth. It is laughable that FoxNews brands itself as fair and balanced. It is not fair, it is not truthful, and it definitely is not balanced.

MSNBC while having an affinity for liberal viewpoints unlike FoxNews' propensity to misinform, bases its arguments and news on verifiable factual information. A comparison of the commentary and the factual supporting information of FoxNews commentators (Glenn Beck, Bill O'reilly, Sean Hannity) versus MSNBC commentators (Chris Matthews, Ed Schultz, Keith Olbermann, Rachel Maddow) is simply astounding. Usually a simple Google search on information presented by FoxNews commentators is easily refuted within seconds. In fact, MSNBC commentators make it a sport to refute them factually and constantly.

Rachel Maddow, a staunch liberal never ceases to amaze me with the depth of her research on every piece she presents. One of her signature pieces[36], a comparison of the depth of legislation and policies successfully achieved by President Obama in 18 months relative to President Reagan in 8 years gave great pause. It was such a well presented piece that President Obama used her piece[37] almost unchanged at the Netroots Nation's Convention in Las Vegas.

---

[36] Rachel Maddows comparison of Reagan & Obama's in a compelling form (http://bit.ly/9CI6eB)
[37] Video of Obama's address to Netroot Nation using Rachel Maddows piece (http://bit.ly/9dtXjz)

Netroots Nation is the body of progressive voices and bloggers.

During the healthcare debate Rachel Maddow was the journalist that presented the most in-depth research to refute Republican outright lies about reconciliation[38] as well as about their hypocrisy on policies[39] they no longer support after supporting them. I find myself partial to Rachel Maddow because of how she ties the facts visually in an entertaining yet effective way. Interesting enough inasmuch as Rachel Maddow refutes the lies of the Right, she just as forcefully go after the sheepishness or disingenuousness of the left when applicable. If more in the news media took her lead and spent the time researching as opposed to reciting political talking points, Americans would be much better able to come to intelligent conclusions.

CNN attempts to be the bastion of objectivity. In the process most of its anchors treat information and political policies from all sides as if they are meritorious. CNN as a news station tend to allow each side to present their talking point, provide minimal

---

[38] Video refuting reconciliation misinformation (http://bit.ly/a7GqnC)
[39] Video exposing Republican hypocrisy (http://bit.ly/aKLOld)

challenge and let the viewer decide. CNN has more faith in its viewers' desire or ability to do their own research on political issues.

Rick Sanchez, Tony Harris, and Kyra Phillips tend to break the CNN mold however subtly. Rick Sanchez seems to buck the CNN mantra by being more challenging on those he interviews. In his own sneaky way I have watched him set many a trap that the interviewee has walked into and make news.

Tony Harris interviews in a fashion that challenges all sides and is always well prepared to provide an alternate viewpoint to prevent complete spinning of the viewer. Tony Harris interview of Shirley Sherrod, the Department of Agricultural employee who was fired after the Right Wing doctored tapes to make her appear racist, was real active journalism. His interview did not assume Mrs. Sherrod guilt or innocence but allowed the interview to reveal the real story on live television.

Kyra Phillips always brings an unbiased perspective by forcing the interviewee to say more than they intended to say. She asks relevant questions and challenges spin quite often. Unfortunately lately she has not been afforded interviews with any substantive figures in the political debate.

CNN must be given kudos for establishing a solid platform[40] that enable the average citizen and citizen journalist the ability to submit news & reports whose newsworthiness is determined by producers. In these times where media research budgets and personnel are under stress, this news "wiki" type news platform presents an excellent opportunity for CNN to have its tentacles all over the world in an economical fashion.

CNN iReport gives CNN the ability to get an empirical pulse of the population. I have been a CNN iReporter for a couple of years and have watched its growth and changes. The young producers and writers at CNN iReport if given the opportunity could revolutionize news and make it more attune to what the American citizenry really expects out of news, how news actually affects them. Team CNN iReport (David Williams, Henry Hanks, Katie Hawkins-Gaar, Christina Zdanowics, Lila King, Rachel Rodriguez, Nicole Saidi,...) are doing a great job in positioning this new platform. One can only hope that it is allowed to develop and change to suit the political, social, and entertainment climate.

---

[40] CNN iReport (http://ireport.cnn.com)

The news departments of the major over the air stations (ABC, CBS, NBC) provide mostly a narration of the news without real in depth analysis. I find the Sunday morning news programs disconcerting in that there is little in-depth analysis and the political guest are very adept of spinning and providing nothing but mostly unchallenged talking points.

Unfortunately, many of the networks and shows that provide factual and refuting information do not have the penetration of the misinformers (FoxNews & Right Wing Talk Radio).

Let me be clear. The Right Wing echo chamber that includes all of Right Wing talk radio and FoxNews is a clear and present danger to our democracy. A democracy requires truthful dissemination of news and information.

The White House finally challenged FoxNews back in September 2009 on its blog[41]. They further went on the Sunday Programs

> *White House senior adviser David Axelrod said*
> *Sunday that the Fox News Channel is "not really*

---

[41] Whitehouse blog challenging FoxNews (http://bit.ly/cSwClN)

a news station" and that much of the programming is "not really news."

"I'm not concerned," Axelrod said on ABC's "This Week" when George Stephanopoulos asked about the back-and-forth between the White House and Fox News.

"Mr. [Rupert] Murdoch has a talent for making money, and I understand that their programming is geared toward making money. The only argument [White House communications director] Anita [Dunn] was making is that they're not really a news station if you watch even — it's not just their commentators, but a lot of their news programming.

"It's really not news — it's pushing a point of view. And the bigger thing is that other news organizations like yours ought not to treat them that way, and we're not going to treat them that way. We're going to appear on their shows. We're going to participate but understanding that they represent a point of view."

White House Chief of Staff Rahm Emanuel said on CNN's "State of the Union" that Fox "is not a news organization so much as it has a perspective."

"It's not so much a conflict with Fox News," Emanuel told John King. "I suppose the way to look at it and the way … the president looks at it, we look at it is: It's not a news organization so much as it has a perspective. And that's a different take. And more importantly, is not have the CNNs and the others in the world basically be led in following Fox, as if what they're trying to do is a legitimate news organization … (7)

Again, FoxNews and Right Wing radio are a clear and present danger to our democracy. Their misinformation documented throughout many reputable blogs does incalculable damage to our body politic because those predisposed to believe the misinformation become reactionary on said bad information. As I write this in Starbucks I am speaking to a man who is 61 years of age and because of the information he is hearing about the viability of Social Security and Medicare because of Healthcare Reform, in his words "Obamacare", he is considering taking his Social Security benefits and Medicare benefits at 62. Moreover he is unaware that because of Healthcare Reform he will qualify today to get affordable healthcare insurance even with any pre-existing conditions. This misinformation causes ill-informed American citizens to make bad decisions that will ultimately materially affect them for the rest of their lives.

That news organizations and Talk Radio are causing a large base of our gullible population to make these decisions are evil. To think that the Right attempts to hold on to the mantra of moral superiority over the population at large when the policies by their very nature cannot be considered but selfish and materialistic lends itself to ridicule.

It is unfortunate that the reputable news organizations like the New York Times, ABC, NBC, and CBS do not more forcefully challenge FoxNews' behavior. One can only wonder if this is the equivalent to the "Blue Code of Silence" or "Blue Line of Silence where police officers refuse to report against fellow officers. The Mainstream Media (MSM) that the Right Wing continuously accuses of being liberal is so fearful of that accusation that they bend over backward to err on the side of the Right Wing.

The lack of unbiased coverage in the news effected the creation of many reputable news/blog portals that while liberal leaning, provide accurate, truthful and generally well sourced information not necessarily covered by the mainstream media.

Daily Kos[42] founded by Markos Moulitsas Zúniga in 2002 with over 2.5 million unique visitors per month and over 250,000 registered users is one of the premiere news organization, community, activist blog site, and news portal that challenge the mainstream media. President Jimmy Carter, Senator Barack Obama, Senate Majority Leader Harry Reid, Speaker of the House Nancy Pelosi, and dozens of other senators, congressmen, and governors are posters of stories directly at the site.

The Huffington Post[43] by Arianna Huffington aggregates mainstream stories. It also has its own reporters that report on their own stories including

---

[42] Daily Kos (http://www.dailykos.com)

[43] The Huffington Post (http://www.huffingtonpost.com)

stories that fly under the radar or stories that many in the mainstream media refuse to cover.

Talking Points Memo[44] (TPM) by Josh Marshall was founded in 2000 after the 2000 Presidential election fiasco. TPM provides breaking news, investigative reporting, as well as high profile guest bloggers.

Media Matters for America[45] is the ultimate non-profit site to refute bogus information and talking point that permeate all media. They systematically monitor a cross section of print, broadcast, cable, radio, and Internet media outlets for conservative misinformation, news or commentary that is not accurate, reliable, or credible and that forwards the conservative agenda. This is done every day, in real time.

Think Progress[46] is a non-partisan blog, a project of the Center for American Progress Action Fund. It provides a forum for the exchange of progressive ideas and policies and often presents the inconsistencies of the Right Wing agenda.

---

[44] Talking Points Memo (http://www.talkingpointsmemo.com)
[45] Media Matters for America (http://mediamatters.org)
[46] Think Progress (http://thinkprogress.org)

Were it not for the above mentioned news portals many stories would go uncovered. A classic example is when David Stockman, one of Ronald Reagan's chief architects of supply side economics and tax cuts, placed the blame of the deficit and economic collapse squarely at the hand of Republican policies over the last 30 years in an op-ed piece he wrote in the New Your Times. This op-ed was written at the height of the debate on whether the Bush Jr. tax cuts should be allowed to expire. Most of the mainstream news organizations disregarded the article which provided relevant information to disprove everything the new Right Wing Republicans were trying to put out. The article was covered over every one of the above mentioned blogs and portals.

The Solution

We are at the point in this country where class warfare is the only solution to our economic problem. Those in the bottom 95% are the builders of this country. They are our teachers, they are our doctors, they are our engineers, they are our sanitation workers, they are our waitresses, they are our small businesspeople, they are our firemen, they are our policemen, they are our pilots, and they are our soldiers. In effect they are America.

Yet, a large percentage of those in the top 5% are methodically and successfully lobbying our politicians with our tax dollars they've ill-gotten in order to pass laws that make it legal for them to pilfer. What is disconcerting is that these guys in the top 5% have been successful in making many of the have-nots actively and vociferously support policies that materially and negatively impact their (the have-nots) own financial well-being as these 5%ers continue to accumulate wealth.

The wealth in this country is unevenly distributed to the top 5% and 1%, not because they are more productive or produce anything of lasting value to society, but because of the structural design of our capitalist society rewarding capital manipulation more so than producing goods and services of societal value. Keep these numbers in your thoughts. The top 1% of the population owns 34% of the nation's wealth, the top 5% owns 58.9% of the nation's wealth, the top 10% owns 71% of the nation's wealth, the top 20% owns 85% of the nation's wealth, and the lower 40% owns less than 1% of the nation's wealth. Income is similarly distributed. The chart that follows illustrates it well.

Wealth & Income Distribution[47]

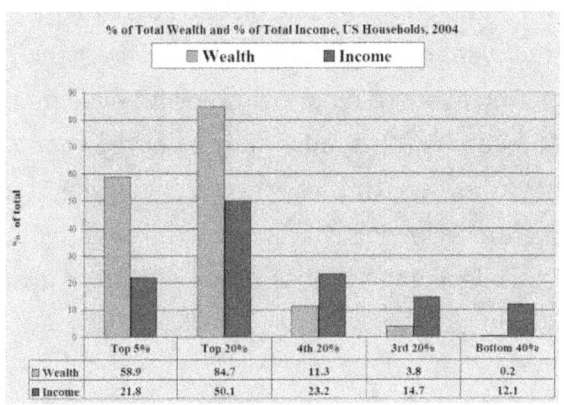

% of Total Wealth and % of Total Income, US Households, 2004

	Top 5%	Top 20%	4th 20%	3rd 20%	Bottom 40%
Wealth	58.9	84.7	11.3	3.8	0.2
Income	21.8	50.1	23.2	14.7	12.1

---

[47] Numerical source is from Federal Reserve Board's Survey of Consumer Finances. Chart found at (http://bit.ly/aYz5PN). (10)

As I stated in an earlier chapter, most working people pay taxes on most of their income while the very rich whose monies are tied to stocks and investments will generally pay a maximum indexed tax to 28%. Moreover, generally no taxes are paid at all on income from municipal bonds. One should also note that most working people pay social security taxes on all their income while the more well off stop paying social security taxes on income over $106,000.

Everything you read about the wealthy being over taxed is fraudulent. Over the last 30 years the wealthy's wealth have been increasing. Over the last 30 years the average American's wealth have been falling or stagnant. It simply cannot be true then that somehow the wealthy is overtaxed or carrying the country. The following chart shows the wealth of most Americans declining as those of the wealthier grow.

Wealth Distribution Over Time[48]

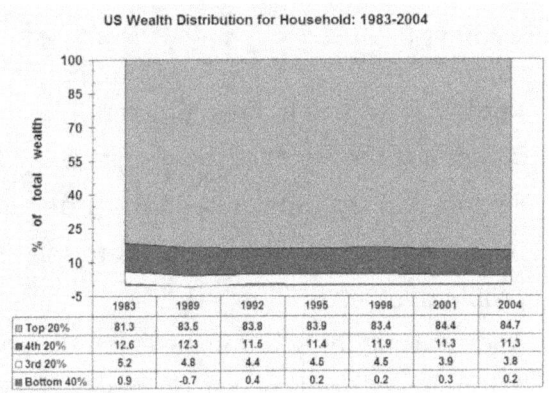

US Wealth Distribution for Household: 1983-2004

	1983	1989	1992	1995	1998	2001	2004
Top 20%	81.3	83.5	83.8	83.9	83.4	84.4	84.7
4th 20%	12.6	12.3	11.5	11.4	11.9	11.3	11.3
3rd 20%	5.2	4.8	4.4	4.5	4.5	3.9	3.8
Bottom 40%	0.9	-0.7	0.4	0.2	0.2	0.3	0.2

The reality is that our capitalist system is designed in such a manner that wealth will progressively be transferred upward. There are no real mechanisms to ensure that equitable distribution is maintained consummate to actual work or productivity. As such societal gain from marginally taxing those who benefited the most from this country providing the platform for said wealth creation, should be seen as a responsibility to maintain a viable society.

---

[48] Numerical source is from Federal Reserve Board's Survey of Consumer Finances. Chart found at (http://bit.ly/aYz5PN). (10)

It is always easy to point out problems. We all intrinsically know what is not working for us. The difficulty comes in

- Recognizing there is a real problem,
- Identifying the effect of the problem,
- Figuring out the root cause of the problem,
- Analyzing the factual possibilities to solve the problem,
- And applying the solution based on the analysis and not necessarily on the politics.

The Right Wing for decades has been just as good as anybody in identifying problems. Because the policies they've supported over the years have generally been the root cause of the problem and because they are unwilling to modify their policies as dictated by mathematically and socially proven facts, they are incapable of solving any of the country's problems. As such they are incapable of governing.

America has a problem. Inasmuch as we continue to pat ourselves on the back as being the best nation in the world, it is important that we recognize that we are at the precipice of a true oligarchy.

The effects of this problem are

- the middleclass losing its wealth
- the middleclass unable to build wealth
- many in the middleclass unable to get a college education
- the middleclass unable to get affordable healthcare
- a poor safety net for the middleclass
- outsourcing of jobs overseas

The root causes of all our problems are

- corruptly regulated capitalism
- corporations, more precisely, the corporate structure.

The solution is actually not difficult if the middleclass educates itself and force the politicians to be of the people as opposed to be of the corporation.

A new paradigm must be defined. In this paradigm free enterprise reigns supreme. What we have now is not free enterprise. We have a corrupted system in which the average American is at the behest of corporate dictates directly or indirectly. In this new paradigm, the individual is free to create his/her own enterprise.

There are three legs to this new paradigm, the government, regulated corporations, and the Individual. All laws must be biased in favor of the individual.

The Goverment

A sustainable Free Enterprise society must have a stable functioning government that ensures citizens are encouraged to take risks to improve society with their discoveries of better products, better solutions, and better services. This entails that if one fails at an endeavor basic humanity is maintained. As a society it should not be difficult to define these. Government by and of the people must manage services that are vital. In other words there should be no tier one profits for these services. Many would want to characterize this as socialism. Some may even want to conflate this as communism in order to inflict fear. I characterize it as humaneness.

Government by and of the people should nationalize banks. After the financial meltdown of 2008 it was proven that corporations operated under the premise of socializing debt and privatizing profits. After-all, the government (we the people), bailed the banks out to prevent an economic collapse. In the process those running these businesses were reaping the benefits of their banks being saved by the taxpayers by awarding themselves big multi-million dollar bonuses. The justification being if these weren't paid these failed business leaders would go elsewhere where they would be better rewarded. Of course there was nowhere to go. In other words they created a false option plausible to some that resulted in them keeping their jobs on the false premise that there were greener pastures out there. During the financial debate these titans of failed finance did not even want a small tax to ensure against their future propensity for failure. Given that in practice the taxpayers are ultimately on the hook, private banks serve no function a civil servant could not perform at a better price.

Government by and of the people must be the health insurer for all Americans. The Obama administration has laid the groundwork for this eventuality even though for political reasons it could not be articulated as such. Inasmuch as insurance companies remain a part of the system, the expectation is that over time they either will be legislated out of healthcare directly or indirectly by forcing enough regulations to protect the average American citizen.

As I stated earlier, there is absolutely no reason to have for profit health insurance companies to pay for basic healthcare needs. A single payer health insurance, the government, without a profit motive is the only efficient solution to our healthcare dilemma.

We purchase healthcare insurance to pool our monies to pay for those of us who may get sick. The insurance company's sole service to us is to pay the bill. This requires no research and development or innovation. As such there is no reason that it requires a profit motive. That being the case makes it undeniable that the sole purpose for the existence of for profit health insurance companies is to create a profit center for an industry; in other words to skim parts of our insurance premiums to deliver to executives, shareholders, and other unnecessary entities. This is nothing but a wealth transfer engine from the average American to the wealthy owners/executives of insurance companies.

As a free enterprise country, companies that provide a product or value should exist; companies whose sole purpose is to skim a profit by denying healthcare, or providing sub-standard healthcare should have no reason in our healthcare delivery. It is for this reason that health insurance companies are a detriment, a cancer to our healthcare system.

Government by and of the people should nationalize the distribution of basic utilities. Earlier this decade the private corporation Enron virtually held California hostage to raise their profits by encouraging suppliers to remove capacity from the market. There is nothing that prevents corporations from creating these false realities. Private corporations have the freedom to sell or not sell. Utilities vital to normal functioning of society should not be left to the devices of private corporations. While it is beyond the scope of this book to detail exactly how this would be done in practice, it is a policy that should be implemented overtime to ensure the "freedom" of the free enterprise system is not held hostage to the few interconnected companies that control the bulk of our utility distribution.

Government by and of the people should ensure that anyone wanting to attend college may do so. In return those getting a college education must be required to serve the nation in some capacity. One's economic condition at birth should not pre-determine one's ability to succeed. America use to be ranked number one in the percentage of the population having a college education. Effective this year we are ranked 12th. It has taken less than a generation for us to achieve this shameful goal. The New York Times article "Once a Leader, U.S. Lags in College Degrees" is telling.

> *The United States used to lead the world in the number of 25- to 34-year-olds with college*

degrees. Now it ranks 12th among 36 developed nations.

"The growing education deficit is no less a threat to our nation's long-term well-being than the current fiscal crisis," Gaston Caperton, the president of the College Board, warned at a meeting on Capitol Hill of education leaders and policy makers, where he released a report detailing the problem and recommending how to fix it. "To improve our college completion rates, we must think 'P-16' and improve education from preschool through higher education." (10)

Over the last 30 years many have fallen into the big government indoctrination trap. We had the Right constantly stating that government is bad. Moreover they ensured that their stewardship of government was in fact bad to make their statement true. At the same time they demonized government they grew it.

Well run big government is not bad but mathematically effective. For services that require no innovation the removal of profits is a net cost benefit to the American citizen. Remember, corporations do not increase their efficiency to reduce costs for Americans; they increase their efficiency to provide better profits and returns to their shareholders. Given that the majority of the wealth in this country belongs to a very small number of people so is the derived profit.

Many of the functions in Iraq from feeding our soldiers to basic building are done by private corporate conglomerates. This reality can be seen in the cost of having contractors feed our soldiers in Iraq & Afghanistan relative to what it would have cost had the military kept these services in house.

Had we increased the size of the military consummate to the wars we want to fight, it would have been much less expensive than paying market prices for products in the front end and paying high salaries and profits in the back end. We have been fed a mathematical impossibility that private sector efficiency provided by large corporations saves taxpayers money. As seen above, this is patently and provably false.

In a free enterprise system large unwieldy corporations should be the exception and not the rule. The reality is that corporations not the government are the largest threat to our freedom. I must reiterate; our government can be replaced in two, four, and six year terms by we the people. Corporations are only responsible to its shareholders and its deeds may or may not be in the best interest of society at large.

Because healthcare insurance is generally provided by corporations, employees of corporations are generally not free to move especially if they have any illness, very common as we age. Moreover because employee provided healthcare insurance from corporations is so much less expensive than getting private individual insurance, it is generally not cost effective to leave the corporation. As such, potential innovations by employees are stifled.

President Obama's Healthcare Reform Bill to some extent levels the playing field in that

- Private insurance will be purchasable from pools that should make it comparable to corporation provided healthcare insurance.
- Denial of healthcare insurance for pre-existing conditions is now outlawed.
- Rescissions, a practice where insurance companies search through your records to find some reason to get out of paying for

procedures or drugs by claiming it is a pre-existing condition is outlawed.

- Importantly, those with college age children must be allowed to remain on parents' policies till the age of 26 making a college education more possible and less stressful.

Unlike the rhetoric, the Healthcare Reform bill actually increases our freedom. Ideally healthcare insurance should be removed entirely from the realm of corporations. As such individuals are free to move as they please. This would then create a real local free market for services from individuals; freedom for the employee, freedom for the individual.

The Corporation

Corporations actively campaign and work against the freedom of workers to unionize. In fact corporations have been very effective in demonizing unions to the point that the very low wage people it is likely to help actively campaign against them. While corporations themselves unionize through organizations like the Chamber of Commerce, and many other trade organizations to maximize their effect on policy, they actively work to deny that freedom to the average American worker.

The Chamber of Commerce, the world's largest business federation, can always be counted on to oppose unions or any policy that provides fairness to the average American employee. Most recently they have come out against The Employee Free Choice Act.

The Employee Free Choice Act

- Allows a union to be certified as the official union to bargain with an employer if union officials collect signatures of a majority of workers.
- Removes the present right of the employer to demand an additional, separate ballot where

over half of employees have already given their signature supporting the union.

- Requires employers and unions to enter binding arbitration to produce a collective agreement at latest 120 days after a union is recognized.
- Increases penalties on employers who discriminate against workers for union involvement.

In effect the law prevents shenanigans and intimidation by corporations. The Chamber Of Commerce opposes the bill on three specific issues[49]

- Eliminating the Private Ballot effectively eliminate private voting.
- Government Arbitration and Control could put government regulators in charge of private business decisions.
- Harsh New Penalties for Businesses would unfairly punish businesses.

The reason for their objection is a stretch. The goal is simply to ensure that the employer maintain the upper

---

[49] See in more detail at the US Chamber of commerce website located at http://bit.ly/ccu7aE.

hand in employee wages giving the employee no bargaining power.

Every worker for a corporation should be unionized in order to protect the interest of workers. It should be noted that ultimately corporations' sole interest is to their shareholders. As such employees are simply cost centers that are continuously squeezed to increase profits for shareholders. This is evident when one sees that wages have been stagnant relative to inflation for the last thirty years while corporate leaders' income have increased by orders of magnitude and the wealth of shareholders continue to march ahead. Earlier in this book I detailed the decoupling of employee wages relative to the corporate leaders.

It is in corporation's best interest to outsource manufacturing jobs. It is fact however that it damages the average American job and job prospect. It was best said by Professor of Finance Rory L. Terry at Fort Hays State University.

> *A great deal of effort is being expended to convince us all that the outsourcing of jobs under the rubric of free trade is a good thing. I would like to discuss some of these arguments.*

Our labor force is not better trained, harder working, or more innovative than our foreign competitors. The argument that we will create new jobs in highly paying fields simply is not true. We have no comparative advantage or superiority in innovation. To assume that we are inherently more creative than our foreign competitors is both arrogant and naive. We are currently empowering our competition with the resources to innovate equally as well as we. Consider the number of new non-native Ph.D.s that leave our universities each year; consider our low rank in the education of mathematics and the sciences; and consider the large number of international students enrolled in our most difficult technical degree programs at our most prestigious universities.

Most of our best, high-paying jobs can be exported.

- doctors (even surgeons)
- mathematicians
- accountants
- financial analysts
- engineers

- *computer programmers*
- *architects*
- *physicists*
- *chemists*
- *biologists*
- *researchers of all types*

Our trading problem is an externality

An externality exists in economics any time there is a separation of costs and benefits, and the decision maker does not have to incur the full cost but receives the full benefits of the decision. The fact is, there is no economic force, no supply and demand equilibrium, no rational decision process of either business or consumer, that will make an externality go away. Classic examples of externalities are when a business dumps toxic waste into a nearby river and the downstream residents incur the costs of cancer. The business is able to lower its costs and pass those lower costs on to its customers, and never pay for the treatment of the cancer patients. We have laws in this country against dumping and pollution because they are externalities -- they require a legislative solution.

Cost reductions and other benefits provide a strong incentive to outsource jobs. *A company that decides to move its production overseas cuts its costs in many ways, including the following:*

- *Extremely low wage rates*
- *The circumvention or avoidance of organized labor*
- *No Social Security or Medicare benefit payments*
- *No federal or state unemployment tax*
- *No health benefits for workers*
- *No child labor laws*
- *No OSHA or EPA costs or restrictions*
- *No worker retirement benefits or pension costs*

Besides cutting costs, there are other benefits to exporting jobs, including the following:

- *Tax incentives provided by our government*
- *Incentives from foreign governments*
- *The creation of new international markets for the company's products (which ultimately empowers the company to turn a deaf ear to this country's problems and influence)*
- *The continued benefits of our legal system and the freedoms that we provide*

The net effect of all of this is lower costs, higher revenue, higher profits, higher stock prices, bonuses for management, and the creation of wealth for a subclass that benefits from low taxes at the expense of the rest of us.

The costs of the decision to outsource are not borne by the decision maker. *As a society and as a country, we experience many costs from outsourcing, including the loss of jobs, social costs, higher costs of raw materials and loss of* *national sovereignty. Loss of jobs reduces the tax base, creates high unemployment benefit costs, and raises the cost of government retraining programs. Displaced, unemployed workers have higher rates of child and spousal abuse, alcoholism, bankruptcy, divorce, etc. As China and India and other large populations grow, they demand huge quantities of oil, gas, steel and other basic raw materials. These costs are born by all of us -- every time we fill our gas tanks, for example. And as a nation, we lose our ability to make independent decisions that are in our best interest when we are dependent on foreign debt and foreign manufacturing. This is a classic externality. (10)[50]*

Professor Terry is absolutely correct. He wrote the preceding in 2004 and the results today are ever so visible. We have allowed corporations to blindly convince us and our government that outsourcing was in our best interest. Inasmuch as we saw steel factories closing, textile industries closing, machine shops, and

---

[50] Reprinted with permission from Dr. Rory L. Terry of Fort Hays State University

just about every other type of manufacturing disappearing, we continued to drink the cool aid.

It is a myth that corporate profits spur innovation. The innovators in corporations are usually salaried engineers and innovators and since most corporations do not particular share profits it is the investor in most companies that reap the reward of employee generated profits. This is a very import statement so I must restate more clearly. Corporate profits absolutely do not spur innovation. Profits by individuals and small businesses in which the innovators have a real stake in the success or failure of the enterprise spur innovation.

Innovation does not come from monolithic thinking. As such the only difference between big government and big corporation is that while the big corporation is solely profit driven irrespective of the service provided, the government is not. As such government that taxes fairly is not an upward wealth transfer engine.

Think about how many corporations actually grow. Corporations with the help of investment bankers search out small companies (real free enterprise companies) that are innovating. They absorb them and control the disposition of the innovation to maximize profits for the stockholder. In the process those who make the most out of the deal had nothing to do with the creation of the newly innovated product or service. In effect the innovation, blood, sweat, and tears are provided by the free enterpriser. The corporation then absorbs the free enterpriser and provides maximal gain to passive shareholders watching their investment grow on some computer screen.

Corporations by design have no morality. While taking a short coffee break from writing this book I saw former Republican Senator Fred Thompson, an AAG spokesman hawking reverse mortgages. He says:

> *"Hi folks, I am Fred Thompson. Now like me you probably heard a lot about reverse mortgages but weren't quite sure how they worked or whether they would be the right financial solution for you. Well take my word for it and hundreds of thousands of other Americans who have used the Government Insured reverse mortgage as a safe effective financial tool. If you are 62 year or older and own your own home, give AAG a call and find out how a reverse mortgage can help you. I am extremely proud to be associated with AAG, a national*

reverse mortgage lender that is helping seniors overcome their financial worries and live the lives they've dreamed. Why don't you find out more by calling AAG today? Find out how much call you may qualify for today."

My first thought was how could a former Senator, a senior, a person who likes to tout morality be so callous to entice the elderly to splurge their wealth away. Most Americans have a large portion of their wealth in their homes. Having some wealth to transfer to one's offspring helps the next generation to the next financial level.

Unfortunately, yet another financial instrument designed to use the ignorance of the average American citizen's knowledge of our economic system to donate their money up the wealth tree to the rich. At the end of the reverse mortgage's term, the elderly is left without an asset to transfer to their offspring at the time of their death.

Corporations must be strictly regulated to ensure that their operations are not detrimental to the population at large. The BP oil well spill presents a classic example. Whereas Norway and Brazil requires an acoustic trigger in addition to other forms of triggering the blowout preventer, such a unit is not available on US wells in the gulf. Oil companies questioned the $500,000.00 cost. Our government acquiesced to the oil companies. The result is likely the largest oil spill in US history and the 2nd largest oil spill in the world.

Corporations' stakes in our lives are too large not to be heavily regulated.

- Are hormones fed to cattle affecting the growth patterns of our children? Corporations should be responsible to prove conclusively it is not the case.
- Are the drugs that we all ingest daily that we ultimately flush into our rivers having an effect on flora and fauna? If it is the case cost/benefit analysis by corporations should be required.
- Shouldn't provable cancers and other diseases caused by corporate waste be mitigated either with an industry tax to defer medical expenses and regulation to cleanup? These must be explored.
- Should corporations be allowed to outsource components and services used in our defense

departments and other areas vital to our national security? Absolutely not.

- Should we allow corporations to knowingly lie over the airwaves? Absolutely not. Whether it is news or commercials, lying over our national airwaves should not be allowed. They are a danger to the functioning of society. I believe Right Wing Talk radio and FoxNews are directly responsible for making a large section of our citizens ignorant to many issues by distorting or outright lying. A misinformed society is a danger to our democracy.

Many will assert that tight regulations would be bad for business. I have no doubt that in the short term the change to making corporations responsible would take its toll. However over the long term society will gain.

Our current policies towards corporations are usually reactive. We have allowed them spread the false narrative that regulation is bad and adversely affect employment. Interesting enough the employment pictured does not reveal that to be true.

The Individual

In several articles I've written in my local newspaper and on several blogs I have tried to articulate that our economic system is designed to give the semblance that the average American with hard work and perseverance can move up the economic tree and accumulate wealth. Generally this is the exception. For most meaningful economic progress is but a dream.

Many of the middleclass have been coerced into the belief of the infallibility of the stock market over time and as such they should be duly invested. While this may be true for the professional investor and the wealthy that have the capital to design option trading instruments like collars or credit default swaps, the average investor tends to be burned badly by downturn after every bubble.

We need not forget what happened to many average investors with the busting of the dotcom bubble and then the housing bubble in less than ten years. Many who thought they would be retiring comfortably at 65 now will likely be working into their 70s or till they die.

Interesting enough those who caused this pilfering are doing fine. In fact many have recovered their losses with the undulation of the market in effect profiting from the average investor trying to buy into a sucker stock rise.

Many have faith in the market as if it is infallible. If we were to assume that the market is self-correcting, periods of self-correction without government as an intervening force makes for great suffering via poverty and loss wealth for the masses. Depending on the length of correction, the potential of an entire generation or more could be lost.

The reality is that we need our economic system and government to be biased towards the individual. Capitalism as we implemented does not serve the individual well. As opposed to capitalism being the tool used to better the individual, the individual has become the tool.

We outsource because we can maximize capital appreciation. In the process the individual loses a job.

We maximize capital appreciation by ultra-low taxes. In the process the individual gets fewer services and is responsible directly or indirectly for a higher effective tax rate that causes larger marginal burden.

We import cheap natural resources like oil as opposed to finding local alternatives. This maximizes capital appreciation necessitating a disproportionately large military to either keep exporting countries in check or ensure shipping lanes remain open. The effect is a smaller potential employment base for the individual.

None of these things happen in a vacuum. The individual is paramount in a representative democracy with a free enterprise economic system.

A functional democracy requires an informed individual, an informed citizen. In addition to being informed, our democracy demands that the informed citizen be engaged.

Corporations have been able to effectively purchase Congress because of a disengaged and uninformed citizenry. In the process they've taken control of the airwaves and used it as a tool of indoctrination. It is for this reason that otherwise intelligent citizens continue to vote against their own interest.

It is the duty of every citizen if we are to remain the great nation we are to ensure that every politician elected will promote policies beneficial for the individual and small businesses.

It is the duty of every citizen to demand that elected politicians do not hide behind rhetoric and cute sound bites without substance.

It is the duty of every citizen to be educated outside the prism of any one media source. It is a must that all information is verifiable.

I have been critical of the capitalist and corporate structure as implemented in America because it has been unsuccessful in creating an environment where wealth & income is equitably distributed based on one's work and productivity instead of simply one's ability to control the movement and manipulation of capital. That said, the individual, the citizen is partly responsible for many of our ills because of shear willful ignorance.

We cannot expect a vibrant US manufacturing sector if we purchase mostly foreign goods when an American alternative is present. We cannot complain about the government being bad, corrupt, or ineffective if we do not educate ourselves on the issues and elect those capable of addressing issues as opposed to those that have the best one line easily understood sound bite. We cannot allow ourselves to be swayed by corporate designed news whose sole purpose is to create an alternate state of reality in which the metrics we use to discern right from wrong, mathematical fact from mathematical fiction, true morality from a façade of morality, true patriotism from faux patriotism, or true prosperity versus a semblance of prosperity to have an effect on the sensible execution of our most important right, the right to vote the correct citizens into office.

Make no mistake. While it may seem that the 2008 crisis just began or came suddenly, that is not the case. Our gullibility to believe Right Wing politicians at face value for the last 30 years have severely damaged this nation.

Conclusion

George Carlin, one of my favorite comedians taped a special called "Life is Worth Losing" at Beacon Theatre in New York City for HBO®. A friend sent a three minute snippet to me that I will cite almost verbatim. Please forgive me for leaving the explicative language in the passage but it gives necessary context of the American worker in its graphic gravity.

> *There is a reason why education sucks. It is the same reason it will never be fixed. It will never get any better. Be happy with what you've got. The owners of this country don't want that. The real owners, the big wealthy business that control all things and make all important decision not the politicians.*

> *The politicians are put there to give you the idea that you have freedom of choice. You don't. You have no choice. You have owners. They own you. They own everything. They own the important land. They own and control the corporations. They've long since bought and paid for the Senate, the Congress, the State Houses, and the City Halls. They've got the judges in their back pockets and they own all*

the big media companies so they control just about all the news and information you get to hear. They've got you by the balls.

They spend billions of dollars every year lobbying to get what they want. Well we know what they want, more for themselves and less for everybody else. I will tell you what they don't want. They don't want a population of citizens capable of critical thinking. They don't want well informed, well educated people capable of critical thinking. That does not help them. That is against their interest. They don't want people who are smart enough to sit around the kitchen table to figure out how badly they are getting fucked by a system who threw them overboard thirty fucking years ago.

You know what they want? They want obedient workers. People who are just smart enough to run the machines and do the paperwork and just dumb enough to passively accept all these increasingly shittier jobs with the lower pay, the longer hours, the reduced benefits, the end of overtime, and the vanishing pension that disappears the minute you go to collect it.

And now they are coming for your social security money. They want your fucking retirement money. They want it back. So they can give it to their criminal friends on Wall Street. And you know something, they'll get it. They'll get it all from you sooner or later because they own this fucking place. It's a big club and you ain't in it. You and I are not in the big club. By the way it's the big club they use to beat you over the head all day long when they tell you what to believe, what to think, and what to buy. The table is tilted folks. The game is rigged. And nobody seems to notice. Nobody seems to care. Good honest hard working people, white collar, blue collar, it doesn't matter what color shirt you have on. Good honest hard working people continue, these are people of modest means, continue to elect these rich cocksuckers who don't give a fuck about them. They don't give a fuck about you. They don't care about you at all. Nobody seems to notice, nobody seems to care. That's what the owners count on; the fact that Americans will probably remain willfully ignorant of the big red, white, and blue dick that's being jammed

up their assholes every day. Because the owners
of this country know the truth is called the
American dream because you have to be asleep
to believe it.

I've always liked George Carlin for a good laugh at
society. I had not seen this special and it was quite
funny that I was sent this clip as I was finishing up this
book. In graphic comedy he is expressing a reality that
most American fear believing yet every chart and
eventuality illustrates it is truer than simple negative
sarcasm.

I am a proud self-employed business man that believes
in the free enterprise system. I believe every living
American deserves the same opportunity to succeed. I
believe government, specifically good effective big
government is necessary to counteract the ills of
corporations.

We must keep in the back of our minds that the
government is us. We the people elect those who
represent government to serve us. Inasmuch as we
complain about lobbyist controlling Congress, their
effect is only as good as our ability to allow them to

use corporate media to deliver propaganda to convince us to vote against our own interest.

We have been voting against our own interest for years. In 2008 President Obama was elected with the expectation that he would change the cronyism that is Washington and finally have the voices of the masses heard. Unfortunately President Obama while passing more groundbreaking legislation in his first 18 months than any other president since FDR, the amount of legislation needed to undo 30 years of political pilfering is monumental.

Interesting enough the corporate media has been successful in demonizing policies beneficial to 98% of Americans. If the 2010 elections prove disastrous for progressives as many believe, the stagnation in Washington will ultimately cause the nation to slide not only into decline but into irreversible third world status given the real competition from BRIC (Brazil, Russia, India, & China).

It would be ironic if the current Tea Party movement becomes responsible for the demise of this nation while the movement it was loosely based on, The

Boston Tea Party was one of the movements responsible for the creation of this country.

America, wake up. Effective today peaceful class warfare must begin to ensure this great nation remain a democracy with every single American having the opportunity to succeed. It begins with educating oneself independent of influences whose ulterior motives are to mislead for the gain of few.

Dedications & Acknowledgements

This is my first published book and I am dedicating it to the memory of my father Egbert Willies. This year I unexpectedly lost my father. I told him a few months ago that I was writing a book and he said he knew exactly what I was going to write about. He saw that I was gravitating from my interest solely from my software development to a more active role in the political discussion. After I did several reports on CNN's iReport mostly on politics as well as maintaining my blog "As I See It"[51] & "PoliticalTruths.info"[52] he said the writing was on the wall. He was right. My father had complete faith in every project I worked on from my years in college to my years in the private workforce. More importantly he was one of the few who had an undeniable faith in my business success when I started my software development company back in 1989. The fear of not living up to that faith is one of the factors that ensured my business success. I miss my father dearly however because of him I am a better son to both him and my mother, a better husband to my wife, a better father to my daughter and a better brother to my two sisters.

---

[51] As I See It Blog (http://EgbertoWillies.com)
[52] PoliticalTruths.info (http://PoliticalTruths.info)

No man is an island. A man is but a reflection of all those he is engaged with. In that light I thank my wife Linda Willies for always being there for me. Firstly she gave me the most wonderful daughter. Secondly when I quit a well-paying job at NASA to start my company she calmly said "Go ahead and do it. You know you need to work for yourself. Anyway, I've been poor before so if we need to move into an apartment that I can afford with my job we will". That type of faith and support is all a man needs to succeed at anything.

I thank my daughter Ashley Willies for keeping me grounded, for constantly challenging me, and for being an all-around great daughter, and ensuring I remain working to pay for her likely 10+ years of college tuition.

I thank my mother Norma Willies-Devonish for my formative years. To this day I attribute my morals to the little voice I still hear ensuring that I do the right thing.

I thank my two sisters Clara Willies-Gill and Dr. Lindia Willies-Jacobo for always believing in me and always being there for me.

I thank my cousin Hector Roberts in Panamá City, Panamá for always being there for me especially with the support he gave me when my dad passed away.

I thank my good friend CJ Lucky for being the big brother I never had. He was the first independent businessman I had a close relationship with and his business acumen was invaluable.

I thank Jerry Pace, a co-worker at NL Industries & NASA for having the faith in me to jointly form a company to design and build an oil well logging system that afforded me the pivot point to create my own company.

Bibliography

1. **Stockman, David.** Four Deformations of the Apocalypse. *New York Times.* [Online] July 31, 2010. [Cited: August 1, 2010.] http://nyti.ms/bkIq0A .

2. **Johnson, Simon.** The Quiet Coup. *the Atlantic.* [Online] May 2009. [Cited: July 26, 2010.] http://bit.ly/cpvhKn.

3. **Krugman, Paul.** The Market Mystique. *New York Times.* [Online] March 26, 2009. [Cited: July 26, 2010.] http://nyti.ms/b4iACl .

4. **Streitfeld, David.** Biggest Defaulters on Mortgages Are the Rich. *The New York Times.* [Online] 07 08, 2010. [Cited: 07 27, 2010.] http://nyti.ms/cUwmb7.

5. **Nasiripour, Shahien.** Geithner: America Is Less Equal Today Partly Due To Bush Tax Cuts. *The Huffington Post.* [Online] August 4, 2010. [Cited: August 4, 2010.] http://huff.to/9CDoKL.

6. **Krugman, Paul.** The Flimflam Man. *The New York Times.* [Online] 08 05, 2010. [Cited: 08 09, 2010.] http://nyti.ms/cLuGMT.

7. **HERSZENHORN, PETER BAKER and DAVID M.** Obama Signs Overhaul of Student Loan Program. *New York Times.* [Online] March 30, 2010. [Cited: August 7, 2010.] http://nyti.ms/dxt3sl .

8. REPORT: Fox News has hyped phony New Black Panthers scandal at least 95 times. *MediaMatters For America.* [Online] July 16, 2010. [Cited: August 5, 2010.] http://bit.ly/bOubwm .

9. **ALLEN, MIKE.** Fox 'not really news,' says Axelrod. *Politico.* [Online] 10 18, 2009. [Cited: 08 06, 2010.] http://politi.co/aKrPj8 .

10. **LEWIN, TAMAR.** Once a Leader, U.S. Lags in College Degrees. *New York Times.* [Online] 07 23, 2010. [Cited: 08 18, 2010.] http://nyti.ms/c4zqiM.

11. **Terry, Dr. Rory L.** Answers on Outsourcing. *CNNMoney.* [Online] March 12, 2004. [Cited: March 16, 2010.] http://bit.ly/9givuK.

12. **Hodgson, Prof. Dennis.** Wealth Distribution. [Online] [Cited: August 11, 2010.] http://bit.ly/aYz5PN.

Index